MARKETING

THE GOOD, THE BAD, AND THE UGLY

TAG Publishing, LLC
2030 S. Milam
Amarillo, TX 79109
www.TAGPublishers.com

Office (806) 373-0114
Fax (806) 373-4004
info@TAGPublishers.com

ISBN: 978-1-934606-51-3

Text Layout: Lloyd Arbour, www.mynewart.com

First Edition

MARKETING

THE GOOD, THE BAD, AND THE UGLY

SUCCESS, FAILURE
AND THE SURE THING

TOM FELTENSTEIN

"Marketing people often forget that a strategy is only as good as the tactics that accompany it. Tom Feltenstein's brilliant new book should go a long way in helping you add muscles to your marketing strategies."

—AL RIES, CHAIRMAN,
RIES & RIES FOCUSING CONSULTANTS

"Most people expect to find gold in the ground. But Tom Feltenstein's new book, The 10-Minute Marketer's Secret Formula puts solid gold marketing and promotional ideas between two covers of an outstanding marketing read. Anyone, in any business can take away dozens of money making ideas and still have leftovers. It truly is a must read for anyone, especially those with limited budgets, who sincerely want to market better, promote better and make a difference in their community."

—DON DEBOLT, PRESIDENT,
INTERNATIONAL FRANCHISE ASSOCIATION

"Tom Feltenstein is either completely, stupendously, stunningly wrong, or he is a stone genius whose counter intuitive insights will transform the marketing business. I'm betting on the latter. Read this fascinating book and you'll likely to come to the same conclusion."

—TUCKER CARLSON,
CONSERVATIVE CO-HOST, CNN'S CROSSFIRE

"Tom Feltenstein's latest book is a must read for business owners who want to increase sales and profits inside their four walls and in their immediate trading areas. His hands-on, how to-information is an invaluable resource that eliminates the need for any mass media-media advertising. I highly recommend this book if you're serious about growing your company."

—ED RENSI, RETIRED, PRESIDENT/CEO, MCDONALD'S CORPORATION USA;
AND FORMER COO, MCDONALD'S WORLDWIDE

"Most marketers are too stuck and too scared to do stuff that really and truly works. If you're willing to get off your couch and make something happen, this book is the first place to start."

—SETH GODIN, BEST SELLING AUTHOR – PERMISSION MARKETING, UNLEASHING THE
IDEA VIRUS, SURVIVAL IS NOT ENOUGH, PURPLE COW, AND FREE PRIZE INSIDE

CONTENTS

To my two beautiful children,
Andrew and Jennifer,
whom I love dearly.

How much would you pay for tomorrow's newspaper?
This book is your tomorrow's newspaper.

—TOM FELTENSTEIN

FOREWORD

WHY DUMB GUYS MAKE SO MUCH MONEY

By Michael Gerber

I'VE WORKED WITH SOME OF THE DUMBEST guys in the world, top guys, in top companies, both large and small.

And I've watched them make gazillions of dollars, over and over and over again.

How could that be? I asked myself.

What is it that dumb guys know that I don't?

The answer to that question is in this book.

It's an answer that's hard to come by, but one through years of experience Tom Feltenstein has had with some of the dumbest guys in the world.

Dumb guys like McDonald's Ray Kroc and Wendy's Dave Thomas. Guys who didn't go to Harvard, didn't go to Stanford, didn't go to any of the best business schools in the world. Guys who simply went about the business of doing what dumb guys do. Doing stuff that works. Doing what's obvious the minute you look at it. Doing stuff that touches ordinary people in extraordinary ways. And once you see it, once it's explained to you, as Tom does very simply and straightforwardly in this book, over and over and over again like a sledgehammer, whack, whack, whack, you suddenly get the message, which is: Dumb stuff works. Dumb stuff works. Dumb stuff works. And dumb stuff, you will learn in this book, is really, really, really smart to do.

A very smart guy I know asked me how I would go about growing my business if I really set my mind to it. The answer I gave him prompted a reply that all smart guys would give. I said, simply, that if I really, really wanted to grow my business, I would put about 1,000 energized straight commission evangelists on the streets across America. And give them a simple story to tell. And our business would explode with growth.

The guy looked at me like I was a moron.

"Straight-commission salespeople?" he said, incredulously. "What about marketing, what about media, what about the Internet?"

The guy was very, very smart. He knew that straight-commission salespeople are a thing of the past. Like seedy old Bible salesmen going from door to door. He knew that marketing, media, and the Internet are about exposure. And he knew that exposure is expensive, that marketing costs money. Serious money. And it is sophisticated. Seriously sophisticated. And because of that it calls for expensive, sophisticated people to do it. He knew all that, and as a result, he just knew that if it didn't cost a lot of money, and if it didn't call for a lot of really, really smart people to do it, it couldn't be very interesting. In short, the smart guy knew that it would take a lot of money to grow my business, because marketing and media and the Internet require capital, gobs of capital, lots and lots of capital. And unless it costs lots and lots of capital, which is money to any dumb guy I know, it can't be worth very much. After all, if all I had to do was to recruit 1,000 salespeople on straight commission, my business couldn't be a very sexy business. And sexy is what marketing's was all about. Sexy is marketing's middle name. Sexy is what smart guys do.

What good would his education do him if the answer was as simple as the one I gave him?

Tom Feltenstein would know exactly what I was saying.

Those 1,000 evangelists out there on the street, in the neighborhood, calling on the customer—who is, after all is said and done, a real person, a real human being, not a consumer, not a market, not a demographic, not a research statistic, but a really, really real person—well, that would fit Tom Feltenstein's Neighborhood Marketing to a T.

That's what makes dumb guys so smart.

They see the extraordinary in the ordinary.

They see the power of the simple, unvarnished truth.

They see that you don't have to be smart to make a gazillion dollars, you simply have to see the unvarnished truth.

And then do something about it! And it's looking at you every single day. It's the dust on your desk, the paper slopping around on your filing cabinet. It's the blown-out light bulb on your old sign, telling your customer, the guy who drives by, that you're all but out of business, you simply haven't pulled the plug yet.

It's the cheap blue wrinkled sports jacket, long past its prime, that your sales manager wears, just to parody the dress code you proudly created once upon a time when your business was new, when you were dumb enough to be enthusiastic. Almost like saying to you, Here's what I think of your stinking dress code. Almost like saying, Your dress code is dumb. And, of course, it is. Dumb, dumb, dumb.

But that isn't all.

It's the surly waiter, the dirty floor, the menu that once was new but isn't new anymore.

It's the kids you hire, or the really, really smart people you recruit out of biz school, none of them having any idea how smart the dumb guys who make so much money really are—dumb enough to be passionate about the simple, small details of ordinary things that make the difference in an ordinary world, in which dumb things done well outdo all the smart things done badly, every single time, and by a mile.

And best of all, it doesn't take a smart guy to do it.

No, dumb's the ticket, as far as I'm concerned.

And believe it or not, ladies and gentlemen, Tom Feltenstein is about the dumbest guy I know.

Enjoy.

Michael Gerber

You are here to get your answers questioned.

TOM FELTENSTEIN

PREFACE

About ten years ago I wrote a book called T*The 10 Minute Marketer's Secret Formula* that was the foundation of my view that to really market, it had to be on a personal level in our own neighborhoods. I started that book with the words: WE LIVE IN INTERESTING TIMES. That is still true, only it is much more interesting than ever before. In the last decade we have seen the advent of life altering social media platforms including Facebook, Twitter, and YouTube just to name a few. The world has drastically changed in some ways, but in others it remains stubbornly the same and my job as a marketer is to make sense of this exciting, and oh so confusing, time for business owners.

It is funny that in all my travels, which include many, many speaking engagements on the subject of marketing, I'm often asked, "What's new?" What new and different ideas do I have to offer today's business owners as they struggle to navigate this new and often intimidating world of integrating their marketing with these new social media platforms?

My response is this: **nothing.** Not because there aren't new and creative ways to market – there are thousands that pop up every day - but because the ideas and principles that make you a success *aren't new*. The platform may be new. The delivery may be new. Even the business itself may be new. But the basic principles of reaching consumers and motivating them to buy are the same.

Now I know that some of you don't want to hear that. Tough. Business is tough and getting tougher all the time. There are hundreds of marketers (maybe even thousands) that will gladly sooth your ego and put a big hole in your pocket while doing nothing for your business. I'm not one of them. Make no mistake, good advice isn't cheap but it's important to note that paying for advice and actually taking it are two different things.

One of the reasons I wrote *The 10 Minute Marketer's Secret Formula* was that I'd met so many business people who were spending too much time *prepping* for great marketing, but not enough time actually *doing* great marketing. It was as if there was a collective failure to launch and I thought it was high time someone start the countdown.

Now the world is even more confusing, and with so many options it is easy for business owners to feel overwhelmed. Compounding this issue are many 'social media specialists' – some of whom have no idea that basic marketing principles exist and that they work for every avenue of marketing, including social media.

Just because something is new or different does not mean you need a whole new method of marketing, it just means that you must tweak the content and delivery to the various outlets so the consumer understands that your message is still the same.

When I first talked about the idea of Neighborhood Marketing it was in the context of concentrating your efforts on a specific neighborhood, and that is still true. What has changed is that the definition of 'Neighborhood' is much more broad and inclusive. You may have a physical neighborhood, but you can also have a Twitter neighborhood, a Facebook neighborhood, a YouTube neighborhood and so on. There are even entire businesses that have no physical location at all and exist solely in cyberspace, yet they can still employ many of the same neighborhood marketing principles I talk about to maximize their marketing.

The core idea is about concentrating your efforts on specific neighborhoods (whatever those may be) and then making sure your message is delivered only to the people most likely to be your customers. It's about an attitude and a way of engaging your customers that distinguishes you from the competition. It is a business philosophy, a management discipline, and a system for running a business with one prime objective: to satisfy the wants and needs of the customer which, in turn, delivers exactly what you want—fame and fortune for your brand.

Quite simply, it is your entire business, seen in terms of its final result, from the customer's point of view.

This book contains a lot of expanded and updated material from *The 10 Minute Marketer's Secret Formula* and outlines for you the powerful principles that make Neighborhood Marketing the incredibly potent tool that it is across a broad spectrum of today's possible marketing platforms. It's a proven system, and it will build your top-line sales quickly and profitably.

I have said it before and it is still true: There's nothing new under the sun. If you and I were to take a walk back through history, we would find countless characters who would fit the description of the Neighborhood Marketer. These would-be marketing heroes are the legendary underdogs, remembered for their ability to seize victory from the jaws of defeat. We would see the dominance of Sears & Roebuck back in the wagon wheel days give way to the likes of WalMart for worldwide domination. We would see Ray Kroc's standardized methodology of making burgers turn into 'Billions Served' by McDonald's. We'd see little upstart Southwest Airlines, that gave away peanuts, become a major player among the Goliaths of the airline world. Neighborhood Marketers have been turning conventional wisdom upside down for decades and those that really understand what it's all about will continue to prosper.

While these tremendous success stories may seem like impossibilities for your business, it's important to understand that these were not flukes. The victories of true Neighborhood Marketers are the result of careful preparation and application of the very principles that I'll share in these pages. When you think of these historical giants of marketing, you need to look at the one thing they had in common that really set them apart – and it wasn't the product sold or the amount of money they had to work with. It was the fact that they understood something that their competitors didn't and they used that knowledge to maximum advantage even when 'conventional' wisdom said they were crazy.

Sam Walton knew he couldn't go head to head with Sears back in the 1940s. His solution was to put small neighborhood stores in towns where there was no Sears store. This was at a time when shopping centers in larger cities were becoming all the rage and everyone competing with Sears wanted to be in close proximity to Sears. Walton, however, was convinced this was suicide and instead marketed to those people in each local area which allowed him to grow a large and loyal customer base. Because he chose largely rural regions, Sears mostly ignored him – until it was too late. WalMart soon dominated the discount market and he enticed customers with wide selections and low cost. Now Sears is barely breathing while WalMart marches on.

Ray Kroc knew that the automation and systems within McDonald's stores would allow them to do something that no one else had before – offer inexpensive food, fast. It was something that hadn't really been done before and customers had to be convinced that his food was as good as any sit down meal. By focusing on making that local customer happy, Kroc showed those early customers that they could expect consistency in quality and fast service at any McDonald's and America was hooked. Now, the rest of the world is too with more than 38,000 McDonald's restaurants in 118 countries.

Herb Kelleher founded Southwest Airlines on a very basic idea: to fly customers from point A to point B at a low price and with great customer service. In the 1960s air travel was all about adding extras to justify the price, while people felt more and more like cattle with no other options. Herb latched onto this frustration and entered a packed market as a low cost provider. His competition sneered and wrote his little airline off as a flash in the pan. Now most of them have gone the way of the vinyl record, while Southwest Airlines has a loyal and growing customer base any airline would envy.

Now it's your turn. This book will be your field guide as you navigate the wild world of marketing just as these giants who came before you with nothing but an idea and the willingness to fly in the face of convention. I'll warn you now that the road may take many twists and turns and will not be easy. But whenever things seem hopeless or uncertainly and chaos ensues, this book will get you back on track and help you turn any obstacle or challenge into a victory.

Neighborhood Marketers are scrappy, untiring fighters for their cause. They bounce back from the nips and bites to attack again and again. Feisty and independent by nature, they become fiercely aggressive and highly disciplined, especially when defending their home territory—their own backyard.

Never forget:

It's not the size of the dog in the fight that matters;

it's the size of the fight in the dog.

INTRODUCTION

IT'S ALL LOCAL: THE REMARKABLE GENIUS OF DUMB MARKETING

It's hard to believe now, but ten years ago the idea of guerilla (unconventional) marketing was brand new. The idea caught fire after Jay Levinson wrote a book about it entitled *Guerilla Marketing*, but the ideas weren't new. You have to remember that in the 1980s mass media ruled marketing and many businesses had gotten away from the principles of grass roots marketing that their businesses started with. But as the year 2000 rolled by, businesses were exploring the idea that perhaps mass media such as television, newspapers and radio might not be the only way to get their message out. At that time, cable television was taking over more and more market share, the internet had taken off in a big way and consumers were being bombarded with advertising from every direction. This meant that, with increasing frequency, a small business had little to no chance of being heard above the din, and thus had to get more creative.

The difference today versus ten years ago is that you can't just advertise, you must engage. Consumers are growing used to the idea of having conversations, not just seeing ad copy. They want and will give input, kudos and criticism. We've gone from an age of marketing to an **age of engagement** on a level none could have imagined a short decade ago.

Ten years ago, the Holy Grail was to capture the attention of consumers in a creative way that would last and that often meant long term ongoing campaigns; today it means going viral - even if only for a few days. Just a short few years ago, product manufactures spent months or years to get their product endorsed by Oprah or other celebrities, now it happens in seconds as today's celebrities tweet endlessly about their lives. Never before has consumer opinion had such an immediate and direct impact on business marketing, and its here to stay.

A celebrity or important personality spotted wearing your brand or eating in your food establishment can be seen by potential customers all across the world in minutes and a windfall ensues. Marketers spend hours these days in meetings trying to figure out what makes this new world work and how they can possibly capitalize on it, but I'm about to let you in on the secret: *Engagement*.

Engagement means that you have communicated with your customer in a way that allows them to associate positive emotions with your brand. In short, buying your product makes them feel good. In years past, I've talked a lot about creating positive emotions with marketing and many people (especially in the 80s) thought it was the dumbest thing they'd ever heard. They thought marketing was marketing and emotions were better saved for chick flicks. I had some even tell me that my ideas were "the dumbest excuse for marketing ever made." But they were wrong.

Even 40 plus years ago the most forward thinking marketers understood the power of engagement and creating that positive association. I've got a picture of the late Ray Kroc, founder of McDonald's, and my principal mentor as a young man, taken in the late 1950s. He's standing in front of one of his stores, in the parking lot, with a garden hose in his hand, washing down the pavement.

There are two things about this picture that, in hindsight, strike me as remarkable. At this point in his career, Ray Kroc could understandably have considered this mundane task unworthy of his valuable time. But it was the same story when he was at the helm of a worldwide corporation as when he was running his first store. Ray was the sort of person who took an intense, personal interest in every detail of his business, from running his corporate headquarters to cleaning the parking lot at one of his stores. He was fully and completely alert and thinking every moment how to engage customers for the long term. His philosophy was simple: **It's all local.**

He understood that if you can't win the customers you can reach in your immediate segment of the market (neighborhood) right now, how in the world can you expect to attract new customers and then build that into anything that will last?

The second remarkable thing is that he considered a clean and tidy parking lot such an important aspect of his marketing that he took it upon himself to make sure it got done. He taught me that being a good neighbor is good for business.

Ray Kroc would go on to take that philosophy beyond the boundaries of his restaurants, creating the Litter Gitter, a three-wheeled vehicle that McDonald's employees drove around the surrounding neighborhoods, picking up trash. Kroc wanted everybody in the neighborhood to understand that McDonald's knew that some customers were careless with the wrappers and cups. He wanted to demonstrate to the community that he cared about their neighborhood. He recognized that so much of what we do, we do for the people in our neighborhood. He preached to anyone who would listen that everything sells, even tidy parking lots. To some this would seem like a waste of his valuable time, but his type of 'dumb' marketing is pure genius. Why? Because it gives people a good feeling about your business and that is engagement. He knew it worked then and it still works now.

Each day we see businesses becoming more socially active in their markets. They are supporting children's charities, pets, and are working to 'green' up the plant. They care and are trying to convey that via today's social media just as Ray tried to convey it to the neighbors that lived next to his restaurant more than 60 years ago.

It's all local and everything sells. That's how Ray Kroc took one of the most prosaic product lines imaginable—hamburgers, French fries, and milkshakes— and built a company that today has annual sales of $70 billion.

For the past 40 years I have been on the marketing side of business, from my role as a senior marketing executive working with Ray Kroc, through thousands of clients in every sort of organization. What I've learned, and what I teach and show to hundreds of businesses every year, is that it's all local and everything sells.

To what I learned helping build McDonald's one neighborhood at a time, I have added a new message that is painfully relevant in today's market: mass media advertising is dead. If you can afford to advertise on television, radio, newspapers, and magazines, you are probably wasting your money. If you cannot afford mass media, if you feel like an underdog surrounded by wolves, I've got great news: you don't need a swollen ad budget to build sales, and you can beat the brains out of the competition cheaply and quickly. Mass media advertising today is little more than wallpaper. It's everywhere, it's constant, and it's invisible.

Worse, most mass media advertising campaigns shout over the heads of the customers they seek to influence. My philosophy and my techniques, which have helped thousands of companies increase their sales and build their brands, aim the message to the customers they already have, and the market they are already in.

In this book, the careful distillation of decades of my own work and research, coupled with the experiences and examples of hundreds of my clients, will teach you how to mine the gold that is already in your business. Everything you need to grow your sales, to make your business a leader in your category and your community, you already have. The only market you need to tap is the one that is within a 10-minute drive of your front door, and inside your own four walls.

It's a revolutionary concept as old as the general store of a century ago, when merchants knew their customers' names, addresses, birthdays, even their family successes and tragedies, and when they cared about their communities. A century of bigger-is-better has created an enormous industry, mass-market advertising, that continues to sell the empty promise of easy solutions to marketing problems.

Now I'm sure that right about now some of you are about to close this book. You may be scoffing, skeptical, or just downright angry that I'm telling you the opposite of what you've heard (or be taught) about marketing. I don't necessarily blame you for your disbelief, but if you close your mind and ignore these ideas, don't be surprised if your business shrivels up and dies in the very near future. Remember, only the business people who were convinced that everything they'd been told was wrong went on to great things. You must take the road less traveled to be successful because the road everyone else is on is littered with the bones of small businesses that could have been great, but died trying.

One last example, Toby Keith. Who, you may say? For those not a country music aficionado, he is a popular country artist of the day. So what? He's nobody, right, just some hick with a guitar. After all, country music is less that 14% of the music market in the U.S. so what could you possibly learn from him?

A lot, that's what. In a recent Forbes article it was revealed that Toby Keith's income for the most recent year was $65 Million. That is more than names you may know much better, such as Jay-Z($42M), Beyonce($53M) or even Jennifer Lopez($45M). Not only that, he's worth over $500 Million right now and has no signs of stopping. Is your business worth half a billion dollars? No? Did you think that someone largely unknown to the vast majority of the country could ever amass that kind of income? No? Then listen up.

Toby Keith could be the poster child for Neighborhood Marketing. He started out in a very small segment of the market, but it was a segment he knew well and he worked hard to engage his customers (fans). Over the last 20 years, he's had a number one hit every year and his customers feel that not only does he understand their lives and their struggle, he is one of them. He has a strong, seemingly unbreakable bond with his fans and this has allowed him to capitalize on what would otherwise be a very difficult market. There have been many singers that made a buck and then went their merry way, but few have become a part of their customers lives like Keith has and it didn't just happen. It was focused and intentional and that is how you must be.

You must integrate yourself into the lives of your customers and engage then one by one if you have to. It is only by studying the experiences and techniques employed by other businesses, from the biggest to the smallest, that you will have a new understanding about what business you are really in and how to promote the core strengths and unique selling opportunities within your four walls. It doesn't matter whether you're a multi-billion-dollar company or a corner grocery store—the same principles apply.

THE MISSION

The Neighborhood Marketing mission is to develop single-unit marketing campaigns whose principal focus is rooted in the four walls and surrounding (7- to 10-minute drive or walk time) trading areas.

The Neighborhood Marketing System is a strategic process based on the singular conviction that the first step in any marketing initiative is to leverage the foundational sales drivers within the four walls.

Each individual operating unit is a medium that contains four business-building tools:

1. The internal customer

2. Products and services

3. Database management

4. Internal merchandising

The premise of the Neighborhood Marketing System is strikingly simple, yet powerful in its impact and continuing effectiveness. The only place you can effectively compete with big-budget, big-clout companies and tap the true potential of your greatest profit opportunity is within your own trading area—the customer base that is right in your own backyard. Businesses, schools, churches, community events, even fellow retailers become your promotional allies in building cost-effective tactical programs to capture consumer dollars in your backyard.

CHAPTER 1

THE AGE OF ENGAGEMENT

Eighty percent of all newly advertised products fail.
The manufacturer decides the customer is a fool.
That's why the product fails. People think advertising
is a cure-all.

FRANK PERDUE, PERDUE FARMS

Chapter 1

SEVERAL YEARS AGO BRITISH RAIL, the company that operates most of Britain's rail service, discovered that its ridership had gone into a steep decline. Like many large companies with too much money and not enough creative thinking, British Rail executives turned to their marketing department for a quick and easy solution. The answer: "We need a new ad agency, a new ad campaign."

They decided they needed a marketing blitz that would lure their customers back to the ticket windows. In the process of shopping for a new agency, the British Rail executives trooped off to the offices of a prominent London ad agency to discuss their needs. As they entered, they were met by a very rude receptionist who told them to sit and wait.

They waited.

They waited some more.

After an insulting length of time, an unkempt staff member of the agency led them to a disheveled conference room featuring a table covered with partially read newspapers, stained coffee cups, and plates of stale, half-eaten food.

Again the executives were left to wait. Finally a few of the agency people, carelessly dressed and ill-groomed, began drifting in and out of the room, ignoring the British Rail executives.

When the understandably annoyed executives asked what was going on, they got a curt brush-off and a shrug of the shoulders. The agency people acted as if they didn't care.

Finally the British Rail people had had enough. The head of the delegation vented his outrage—whereupon one of the ad agency executives smiled, approached him, and said:

"Gentlemen, your treatment here at this agency is not typical of the way we treat our customers. In fact, we've gone out of our way to stage this meeting for you. We behaved this way to demonstrate what it's like to be a customer of British Rail. The real problem at British Rail isn't in your advertising. It's your people, your customer service. We suggest that you let us help you fix your employee attitude problem first, before we attempt to fix your advertising."

The British Rail executives were shocked at first, but the agency got the account. It stood out. It proved it was remarkable. The ad people had the courage to point out to British Rail that the answer to their problem was right inside the four walls of their operation. And so is yours.

WE ARE ALL WEIRD

Since the early part of the last century, the world was about automation and production. Fulfilling the needs of the masses with mass produced and distributed product. From 1900 to the year 2000, we were a one size fits all factory oriented world. Since then, just over a decade has passed and that world is slipping away so fast you can almost hear the wind as it rushes out the door. We have shifted dramatically, and very quickly, back to a world where individuals are prized and everyone wants to be heard. The rise of addressable tribes, mini-communities and people obsessed with causes, hobbies and passions is changing politics, economics, marketing, manufacturing and everything else.

The way I see it, you have two choices. You can fight to protect the status quo (and lose) or engage in the most important revolution of our time. That means no more meaningless rhetoric. The old days of telling your customers what they want, how they want it and when they will get it are over! We are now living in a content driven, customer oriented society and the truth is that customers would rather watch cat videos than listen to your empty words and promises. And they can. Instantly, with one click. Which is really scary when you think about it because you have mere seconds to capture anyone's attention.

You don't have any time to waste and every second of meaningless drivel you continue to put out is costing you money. This is a call to action to back away from the rhetoric and really understand and embrace the new business Rules of Engagement.

RULES OF ENGAGEMENT

1. GET A NEW JOB

2. GET OVER YOURSELF

3. YOU'RE A DROP IN THE OCEAN

4. YOU'RE PROBABLY ON SOMETHING

5. ASK: WHAT'S THE INSIGHT – INCITE?

6. FOLLOW DIRECTIONS

7. BE CONTAGIOUS

8. CAFFEINATE

9. ENGAGE THE AUDIENCE

RULE OF ENGAGEMENT # 1

GET A NEW JOB

What do you think your job is as a marketer? I ask that to almost every marketer I meet and almost without fail, they will say something like: "Its about telling the story so the customer gets it" or "Its about engaging people with the idea of our brand and conveying our message." To which I say, "Wrong!" That was your job ten years ago, telling the story; engaging the customer WITH the story. Now it's about engaging people IN the story. It becomes part of their lives, not just something you want them to hear. It is interactive and give and take, not shouting with a bullhorn. This is rule number one because until you get this one rule, you will be spinning your wheels.

RULE OF ENGAGEMENT # 2

GET OVER YOURSELF

I am frequently amazed at the level of arrogance that many marketing directors still have. They honestly think that they decide how customers feel about their brand no matter what the situation. They pompously sit in their nice offices dreaming up new ways to shape their brand so they can 'push' that idea to customers. Obviously they have not yet been humbled by the new rules of engagement.

Rule #2 is Get Over Yourself because the humbling is a comin'. Don't believe me? Ask Carnival Cruise Lines. One engine failure, and suddenly 'The Fun Ship' becomes the floating poo palace and there is no way to get that genie back in the bottle these days. Gone are the days when if something went wrong, you just swept it under the rug and ran more commercials. Customers shape the idea of your brand each and every day with reviews, tweets, posts and all kinds of online interaction. How others see you is important because what a very small number of customers say can be extremely powerful. There are no small PR mishaps these days. They are shared, dissected and many times picked up by the mainstream press before you can park your Beemer and get a latte.

In order to harness the power of marketing in a social media laced world, you must first understand how powerful it really is – and know that same power can be used against you as easily as it can for you.

When you interact with customers you must remember it is a conversation, not a lecture. You have to be willing to share, listen and respond in a very timely fashion.

RULE OF ENGAGEMENT # 3
YOU'RE A DROP IN THE OCEAN

One of the downsides to a world where consumers have all the information they could ever need or want at their fingertips, is that they are drowning in content. Why do you really think those cat videos are so popular? Because it's not as overwhelming as slogging through all the other information out there! I recently heard a speaker say that the deluge of content via the internet is on the way. Well, I've got news for you Buddy, its already here! Just like most things concerning the internet, that is both good and bad. Bad in the respect that there is a lot of competition for people's attention; Good in the respect that you can easily see what is trending at any moment and what types of content are getting attention. This short cuts your learning curve.

There are some very simple guidelines to developing content that will hold customers' attentions. If you have a product, you can develop useful content that customers seek before they purchase. You can answer frequently asked questions. You can show them how to use your products and how well they work, all while encouraging customer reviews that people will want to read. If you think this sounds like an infomercial, then you are right! Even today in the deluged information highway, infomercials still sell product and that should tell you something. It doesn't have to be revolutionary to work.

Rule of Engagement # 4
You're Probably on Something

When I say you are probably on something, I mean you are connected. Almost every single person has some sort of electronic device in their hand most of the day, everyday. Think about yourself. How often are you on Facebook, Twitter, YouTube, Email or just surfing to be surfing? If you aren't necessarily a techie (and believe me I'm not!) you can't ignore the fact that most of your customers are. In a world of smart devices – don't be DUMB! Your message needs to be everywhere and you have to make it accessible.

What does that mean? 70 year old farmers can post a video about growing corn, so you can certainly post a video about your product or service – in fact you should have your own channel so you can post a lot of videos and then share them across all possible platforms. Don't just load it to YouTube and forget it, share it!

Are you on Pinterest? Do you have photos? In case you haven't noticed social media has quickly moved from a mostly text environment to a very visual one so don't leave your customers in the dark. What about you Blog? Yes, you should have one (goes without saying) but you need to share it across all your social media. Auto populate your feeds every time you post so you don't even have to think about it.

One question I get a lot is what to put where. Now its time to put your 'marketing' hat back on. Think about the users of each group and what they are there for. For example, on Facebook people want to be entertained. They are looking for distraction and information so put your best content here. On LinkedIn, users are there for professional networking so put your business content there. All you need to do is think about what the users are on that site for and then match your content to that desire.

Search Engine Optimization has been a buzzword for so long now it makes peoples' eyes glaze over, but it's still important that you optimize keywords for the likes of Google and other search engines. People surf more now than they ever have because they can also do it from their phones – they don't have to sit in front of some kind of old fashioned terminal anymore. Great keywords allow them to find you.

THE THREE "F"S OF SOCIAL MEDIA:

1. Fun
2. Feedback
3. Fellowship

RULE OF ENGAGEMENT # 5

WHAT'S INSIGHT INCITE?

Incite is the creative idea at the heart of every campaign and it is what motivates. Through its basic originality and share-ability, it can propel your marketing farther, faster than you ever could. When you develop effective and creative Incites they can spark movements, transform businesses, expand brands and expose issues. The bottom line is to stop trying to sell something to someone and start understanding how you want your customer to feel. Engage the emotion through the four different types of Incites.

THE FOUR INCITES:

1. Stir Up
2. Encourage
3. Persuade
4. Prompt to Action

RULE OF ENGAGEMENT # 6

FOLLOW DIRECTIONS

Of course you follow directions, don't you? Unfortunatly almost no one does or every company I ever talked to would be wildly successful. In truth, I'd say less that 3% really do what they need to in order to revamp their marketing and engage customers. What I'm about to share is a basic marketing model you can use to decide how and where to spend your marketing dollars. It's simple, effect and it works.

MY 70/20/10 MARKETING MODEL

70% of budgets go toward "blocking and tackling, doing what we know drives business." This means spending money where it is already effectively attracting customers and getting a good ROI.

20% is reserved for innovative ideas that have some knowledge behind them. Like the tactics I've presented here. They are different than what you or your competition are doing and they have a vast amount of experience and knowledge behind them.

10% is dedicated to high-risk, high-reward bets. This can be those creative, outlandish ideas, most of which probably won't work. But the one that does will hit it out of the park so it is important that you budget to keep swinging for the bleachers.

RULE OF ENGAGEMENT # 7

BE CONTAGIOUS

VIRAL IDEAS SHOULD:

1. Inspire
2. Delight
3. Entertain
4. Shock
5. Captivate
6. Illuminate

If only going viral were as easy as catching a virus! But its not. Not that many companies don't actively try to reach this pinnacle of internet marketing success, they do. Its just that they don't succeed very often. Who would have thought Angry Cat would become a viral sensation? Or that a blanket with sleeves would get a viral boost from its cult following and the multitude of spoofs of the product?

Going viral is not really something you can plan on, but if you prepare, then you can allow yourself to be at the right place at the right time to catch interest and then catch flame. While there are no guarantees, there are some definite qualities that viral ideas share. The idea is to create emotional experiences that drive participation.

RULE OF ENGAGEMENT # 8

CAFFEINATE

Your business can't go to sleep, not in this world. You have to be ready at a moment's notice to react and respond to anything whether it be good or bad. Tomorrow is too late! You must answer questions, project positive emotion, update customers on the latest and greatest and even argue sometimes! Remember that engagement is a conversation and it can't be one-sided, or only happen when you feel like it.

DELIGHT IN THE UNEXPECTED

- Modern

- Sophisticated

- Vibrant

- Possible

RULE OF ENGAGEMENT # 9

ENGAGE THE AUDIENCE

As I said at the beginning, this is the Engagement Era. Stop preparing to launch and just do it. Start immediately to converse, inspire and create a movement among your customers. It is what businesses have done since the beginning of time, but now we're just in a different environment. Things have changed, products have changed, businesses have changed, people haven't changed.

Don't fear the new or unknown, embrace the possibilities and be willing to learn.

You don't have to be great to start, but you have to start to be great.

TOP 10 TIPS FOR MODERN MARKETING

1. Segment your services: Twitter (perceptions), Facebook (people), Google+ (passions), Pinterest (pinning), and LinkedIn (pimping).

2. Prepare a great profile: Good photos, full-face, in-focus, no-red-eye, simple and truthful bio.

3. Curate, don't create: It's too consuming to constantly create, so be essential by finding great content.

4. Act like PBS: Curate so much great content people don't mind the telethons.

5. Restrain yourself: Don't promote products or services more than five percent of the time.

6. Candify: Add a picture or video to every post.

7. Respond: Don't simply broadcast; respond as well.

8. Stay positive or stay silent: Winning an argument usually means losing the war.

9. Repeat: Don't be afraid to repeat your best posts. CNN doesn't run a report once. Why should you tweet once?

10. Do; don't plan: Planning is overrated – just dive in and figure it out as you go along.

FACE-TIME MARKETING

The first people you must engage are those in your business. If you can't get them to understand and participate in a conversation, you will never engage your customers. Your marketing messages are conveyed one-to-one: first to your employees, then from your employees to your guests, and finally from your guests to their families, friends, neighbors, co-workers, and social media contacts. Face-time marketing is intimate and personal, the opposite of slick, impersonal, mass media advertising. You start face-time marketing by hiring, training, and motivating your employees, then leading them to go beyond the idea of service and embrace your own belief in hospitality.

Service is mechanical. It's putting the right-size tire on your car, installing carpet right-side-up, writing your airline ticket to the correct destination. It's essential, and it's teachable, but it's not hospitality.

Hospitality comes from the heart. It's the personal connection you make with each individual who comes through your door. It's caring about the customer as a person, not as just another number on the balance sheet.

Mary Kay Ash, founder of the phenomenally successful cosmetics company Mary Kay, understood these concepts better than anyone and built an empire on them. She once said, "Everyone has an invisible sign around their neck that says, 'Make me feel important.'" If your customers posted their expectations on your social media, it would say, "Right here, right now, tailored for me, just the way I like it."

If nothing else, this should convince you that talking at people is finished. Let's start a conversation.

SEVEN LESSONS AT THE CORE OF NEIGHBORHOOD MARKETING

1. It's all local.

2. The heart of Neighborhood Marketing is inside the four walls of your own business.

3. Community involvement is essential to effective Neighborhood Marketing.

4. Trust your people.

5. A good idea doesn't care where it comes from.

6. To make it work from top to bottom, it has to work from bottom to top.

7. Once you deliver a powerful level of service—one that goes beyond the expected—you've made a tangible bond with a customer that no mass media program can achieve.

CHAPTER 2

THE MOST PROFITABLE MEDIUM - YOUR FOUR WALLS

*The only reason to be in business
is to create a customer.*

PETER DRUCKER,
THE FATHER OF AMERICAN MANAGEMENT THEORY

Chapter 2

SANDRA PICKED UP HER BRAND-NEW CAR on a perfect summer day, under a clear blue sky with a cool breeze wafting off the ocean. Ron, the salesman who'd arranged her purchase two days earlier, greeted her at the showroom door with a broad, warm smile and a firm handshake. A waiting assistant promptly took the keys to her dusty, mile-weary trade-in and drove it around the corner, out of sight. Ron had all the documents ready and laid out in the exact order Sandra needed to sign them. As she executed the title, financing, and other paperwork, Sandra enjoyed a freshly brewed cup of coffee and some friendly banter with Ron. In no time at all, her sparkling new silver Lexus was purring at the showroom curb, her new partner in a journey that would take them many thousands of miles.

Sandra settled into the driver's seat, breathed in the earthy scent of the new leather, and eased her new chariot out of the parking lot and into the afternoon traffic. She turned on the radio and pushed the first auto-select button to begin programming her preferred radio stations, the first act of new-car ownership. Her face lit up as her favorite top-50 station filled the air with a tune she was especially fond of. She warbled along as she weaved her way through traffic toward home. When the first commercial came on, she pushed the next select button. A swelling of violins flowed from the speakers. This was her favorite classical station!

Amazing, she thought. She tried the next button and on came her favorite all-news station. The fourth button summoned her husband's favorite sports channel. This was getting spooky. Had technology reached a stage of development that made it possible for a car to read her mind?

She reached home, pulled into her driveway, and immediately called Ron to tell him about this amazing coincidence.

"You wouldn't believe it," she gushed. "I just had to call and tell you. I must be doing something right. Every one of my favorite radio stations was already preselected. What an amazing coincidence!"

Ron chuckled. "That was no coincidence. When a customer buys a new car and we take a trade-in, we check the old radio, write down the stations on the set, and then program the new ones to match."

In that moment, Sandra became a devoted, loyal customer of the dealer and of Ron. And then, for the next two weeks, reveling in the honeymoon with her new chariot, she told everyone she knew about the dealer and what incredible service she'd received with her new car. She shared pictures of the new car and gushed all over Twitter and FaceBook about the wonderful service. Where once she may have reached 30 to 50 people, hundreds saw it via social media.

That's Four Walls Marketing! No expensive newspaper ads, no annoying radio commercials, no slick TV ads. Just the cost of 15 minutes of labor by a mechanic. How many cars did Sandra sell for the dealer?

DO SOMETHING REMARKABLE

My dentist, Dr. Mitchell Josephs, of Palm Beach, Florida, asked me one day if I could brainstorm with him some ideas to grow his practice. Everyone's business is hurting these days, and dentists in particular have been hurt by advances in technology that make tooth decay and gum disease almost extinct. Cosmetic dentistry, with the highest profit margin, is discretionary and not covered by insurance plans. In a bad economy, people don't have teeth whitened, capped, and straightened.

"You've got to do something remarkable," I said. "Now, your hours are Monday through Thursday, nine to five. I want you to be available nine to six, seven days a week. I want you to be available when your competition is closed and whenever your patients want you. I don't want them ever to call and get an answering service or machine. I want you to give them your cell phone number, and I want you to answer it 24 hours a day."

You might have expected him to start whining about being bothered at home, or when he's out to dinner. After all, dentists and doctors are practically gods. But instead he looked at me with a broad smile on his face.

"You know what I do on the weekends? I sit around on my butt and read the paper and watch too much television. I love my work, and I'd rather be doing it and growing my business than sitting at home watching my waist grow."

To him it was an absolutely revolutionary idea. Next we talked about who might have the income in a bad economy to afford cosmetic dentistry. Doctors stay busy through thick and thin, and earn good incomes. Then it occurred to me that doctors can never find time to go see a dentist during office hours because they keep the same hours. When doctors are off duty, so are dentists.

So we contacted the neighborhood hospital and bought their mailing list of about a thousand local physicians. Mailing lists can include snail mail addresses as well as email addresses.

I told him to hire a graphic artist to design a postcard that featured some really upscale veneers, the ones that all the Hollywood actors are getting now. "Find an attractive patient willing to have her picture on the postcard showing her teeth before and after the veneers have been applied. The picture will say it all." You may think that mail outs are passé, but where once people got a lot of junk mail, they really don't anymore, and since this required a visual pitch, it was well suited.

Then I told him to put some text on the card that said, "I'm a health professional, and I know how hard it is for you to find time during the week to take care of your dental needs. That's why I'm open weekends to serve you. Call me anytime on my cell phone, and I'll be happy to see you when you're ready."

I warned him ahead of time that he would have to do a series of mailings and if he were doing it today I would also tell him to post before and after photos on Facebook, Pinterest, a video on YouTube and connect with these doctors on LinkedIn. One little ad won't do it. Statistics show that consumers won't act until they've seen a message between four and seven times. The good news is that with social media you can up your chances of people taking action sooner.

Sure enough, after the fifth mailing he called to tell me he'd gotten his first patient, a neurosurgeon who had $22,000 worth of work done.

The single most important ingredient in a successful business is having a customer. Customers buy to feel good or to solve a problem. Customers want you to be available when they are available. Why are grocery stores open 24 hours? Why is Walgreen's open seven days a week? Because the customer wants them to be open.

I gave my dentist a number of other revolutionary suggestions: Never stand over your patient. Always sit at the same level. Make sure your waiting and treatment rooms are decorated with pleasing colors. The chairs must be comfortable. The magazines need to be updated regularly, not just every three or four years. Four Walls Marketing is all about the environment, the feeling, even the music. Make patients feel they are walking into a cozy living room. Get rid of the dehumanizing intercom patients have to buzz to get in. Have your receptionist sit out in the waiting area where everyone can see and talk to her. Your office isn't Fort Knox.

Always call patients within 24 hours of treatment to ask how they're doing. They appreciate knowing that the dentist cares about them, even if they've only had a cleaning. For the pennies it costs to make that call, the opportunities that follow-up phone calls present are amazing, from defusing a misunderstanding that could cause a patient to go to another dentist to selling other services that the patient thought about after getting home.

I told my dentist to do some research about his patients. "Have your receptionist ask your patients what social media they are on, what magazines or ezines they read, and what print media they read. Then use those outlets to buy mailing lists or post ads. Even The Wall Street Journal sells its mailing lists. Find those people who are in your primary trading area, from their zip codes and via city searches on social media. Then communicate with them. Send them a series of direct mail letters and promotional pieces once a month for seven straight months. Talk about your promotions via social media and answer questions. Start a conversation.

I hear all the time from business people, "I sent out a direct mail piece (or placed an ad) and it didn't work." If you're going to buy a television campaign, are you going to run just one spot? Of course not. Why would you expect a big result from one mailing? Yet most business owners make that same mistake and assume that if it didn't work the first time, it will never work when that's not true. It's all about continuity and social media helps fill in the gaps between ads or promotions to increase the customers' motivation to buy.

Finally, I told my dentist that when he's finished major work on a patient, send a gift each month for the next six months. A fruit-of-the month basket is easy and inexpensive and again, something that people will take photos of and share. Remind the patient that you care, that you're there for him, and turn your customer into a marketing ambassador for your business.

THINK LOCAL

The marketing battlefield has changed. It's critical to downsize your marketing to match your prime market. Your business is a far better advertising medium than newspapers, radio, TV, or billboards. Most of us were taught the mass media theory of marketing: think big. But profits today are being made by those who think small, and the smaller the better. Single store, even for the biggest chains, is the best of all.

Have you ever seen a mass market ad campaign for Starbucks? Not until recently and even then its limited. Paul Newman's food company doesn't advertise. The Virgin Group of companies gets along quite well without much advertising. What about restaurant chains like The Cheesecake Factory, or clothing stores like Tommy Bahama? What about Krispy Kreme and Harley Davidson? No mass media, right? Yet these are some of the most successful marketers in the world.

As you read on, you'll find out how these companies and many others have enjoyed phenomenal success without going broke buying ad campaigns that don't work.

Mass media advertising was developed for another age in another marketplace. That's why I say that face time, the personal touch inside your four walls, beats air time (advertising) every time.

Let's get started.

CHAPTER 3

CHECK OUT THE NEIGHBORHOOD

Strategy is war on a map.

HENRY CANNON, CANNON TOWELS

CHAPTER 3

FOR MANY YEARS, GEORGE GREENBERG, an old friend of mine from West Palm Beach, Florida, has owned an upscale linen store near my home. One day I stopped in to visit and asked him how his business was doing. He complained that it wasn't as good as it had been and he didn't know what the problem was. The economy was bad and he was thinking about letting some of his staff go in order to cut costs.

"That's the worst thing you could possibly do," I said. "Wouldn't you rather increase your sales? You know, just a 2 percent increase in top-line sales is equal to a 10 percent reduction in operating expenses."

George conceded that he'd hate to let anyone go, but he was stumped for ideas. I looked around the place, and the first thing I noticed was that the décor hadn't been updated in about 25 years.

"Yeah," he admitted. "I know it."

I looked at his catalog and discovered it was printed in black and white. I couldn't believe it! He was selling beautifully colored sheets, towels and window treatments, and the message he was sending his customers was stale and flat.

I asked him, "Do you have a preshift meeting every day when you open your store? Do you talk each day for a few minutes about the sales goals you're setting? Do you have an incentive contest for your staff for how many pillows or sheets you're going to sell on any given day?"

You can guess the answer to all these questions. George was in desperate need of a Neighborhood Marketing plan.

First we redecorated and modernized the look of the store. I persuaded him, with much badgering, to spend money on a color catalog. We set up an incentive program for his employees to sell high-margin items, then showed him how to market to his neighborhood.

George got his bookkeeper to do some research and calculate the average sale per customer. It was about $225. He agreed that he'd consider a promotion successful if it would boost the average sales ticket to $250.

I next contacted a local restaurant, Morton's Steakhouse, that catered to the clientele that patronized George's linen store. I asked the manager, "What's your average sale?" It was $60. He told me he'd be pleased with a promotion that added $10 to that.

So we arranged a cross-marketing promotion that worked like this: if a customer came in and spent $250 at George's, she got a $50 gift certificate to go and eat at the Morton's. Morton's agreed that customers who spent $70 would get a $50 gift certificate for George's linen shop.

We put a sign up in each of the businesses so the promotion would have exposure. George's was now advertising for the restaurant, and vice versa. We trained the staff of each business to explain and promote the other business to their customers. The only out-of-pocket cost was the food and the certificates. We did no advertising.

Customers were rewarded only if they spent money in both locations. We exposed a lot of new people to both businesses.

The result was predictable. Top-line sales increased in both stores. In the restaurant, customers who presented certificates usually did so for a special occasion and ended up spending more than they would have otherwise. George's customers felt cared for, told their friends, and became repeat customers. The most essential part of the plan was getting George's house in order BEFORE attracting customers. If you don't then that old décor, stale catalogue and antiquated customer service will be all over social media and do much more harm than good. So you must get your ducks in order.

There really is no magic to building top-line sales. I'm going to show you how to build a killer Neighborhood Marketing plan, and explain the seven key steps to building your top-line sales all while integrating social media.

WHAT IS MARKETING?

Your property has something to do with marketing, as Ray Kroc understood so well. If your employees wear uniforms, that's marketing. The person who sets the schedule (for who works when) is part of marketing.

Every part of your business is marketing. In a restaurant, even the linen is marketing. Fine-dining restaurants discovered that women were complaining about white napkins. Black is a popular fashion color these days. Guess what happens when a woman wearing a black dress or slacks puts a white napkin on her lap? When she gets up from the table, she's got white lint all over her. So now these restaurants offer black napkins. It is a small thing, but every small think matters.

Companies that offer marketing services tell me that when they hire new team members right out of college, they come on board thinking, "Cool. I'm gonna work for a marketing company. I'm gonna do TV commercials and stuff." But that's not what marketing is about. These rookies get a rude awakening when they're put to work crunching numbers. Numbers and data have everything to do with marketing.

Melissa Wilson, a marketing expert I often work with, used to be a general manager in the restaurant business. She recalls, "My managers hated me because I used to create paperwork. We didn't have a lot of forms and systems when I started, and I was having fun with this restaurant building sales. I wanted my superiors to know that I was up 9.3 percent, year over year. I could put it in their faces and say, here it is. Paperwork may be the bane of our business, because we should be out taking care of our customers. But the details, the numbers, are important. It helps streamline what we do and makes our marketing job go easier."

In your business, how do you decide when to schedule a favorite employee? Do you simply plug bodies into schedules? Instead of just taking an employee you like and buying his or her time, you are actually doing a scheduling plan and a purchasing plan. Marketing is no different.

We plan our labor needs by scheduling, we plan our purchasing needs by measuring what we sold last week or last year, and we plan every other aspect of our business.

But what do we do when it comes to marketing? "I have a cool idea." Or we see what somebody else is doing and we copy it.

You would never do that in any other aspect of your business. Suppose you walked into a bank and said, "Business plan? No need for one. We'll just copy what Starbuck's did." After the loan officer finished laughing, would she hand you her bank's precious money? Don't bet on it. Nor should you take on any business activity as crucial as marketing without a well-designed Neighborhood Marketing plan.

STEP 1: GATHER DATA

Yogi Berra, the legendary New York Yankees catcher, coach, and master of the malapropism, once said, "If you don't know where you're going, you might end up someplace else."

The first step of planning your marketing is often the hardest. Gathering data takes time, it's boring and tedious—and it's absolutely essential. You can't choose where you want to go if you don't know where you are. More money has been poured down more drains on more misguided marketing efforts because people didn't take the time to find out what their customers wanted, what their employees were able and willing to do, and what resources they had in their businesses. The Ritz-Carlton Hotels, in spite of the chain's well-deserved reputation for excellence, discovered this phenomenon the hard way. As it does with every aspect of its business, the company spends a lot of time and money on the details, right down to the lush and fresh floral arrangements in the lobby. In its signature properties, when upgrading the bathrooms, Ritz-Carlton insisted on the best and most beautiful décor. The company spent untold millions of dollars in design fees, color-matching, and shipping all the way from Italy the most beautiful green marble and installing it in its guest bathrooms.

After all this expense and effort, the company finally got around to doing some data gathering. Ritz-Carlton commissioned a research study to ask its customers questions about its service, accommodations, and ambiance. The results were astonishing and heartbreaking to Ritz-Carlton executives.

Yes, customers said, Ritz-Carlton does a great job and its hotels are top of- the-line, but guests couldn't care less about the marble and the flowers. They only cared about service, rapid check-in, that sort of thing. And what color did the guests want in their bathrooms? White. They wanted it pure white so they could see it was clean. Ritz-Carlton had spent millions of dollars and thousands of people-hours without asking its guests what was important to them. Big mistake.

SURVEY YOUR INTERNAL CUSTOMERS

One of the hardest concepts to get across to business owners is that your employees and staff are also your customers. You can do all the clever marketing in the world, but if your staff aren't on board, if they aren't engaged and enthusiastic, the results will be unsatisfying.

The first input you want is from all the managers in your business. Create a system, a hospitable work environment, that encourages your managers to speak openly and honestly with you. It's their neighborhood, it's their career, and they should have a sense of ownership in any plan you come up with. Otherwise, they won't help make it effective.

Managers will often find something to complain about. That's okay. Let them complain. Everybody needs to vent, and you need to leave your ego at the door. You want the truth, not a response that makes you feel good. You want a candid evaluation from every internal customer, from your top-line managers right down to the guy who vacuums the floor. What do they really think about the product or service, the pricing, the atmosphere—all of it? Make no mistake, no matter what policy you have at your establishment concerning social media, your staff will share their real feelings and if they can't share them with you in an open and honest discussion, they will share them with the world.

It regularly amazes my clients when they learn that their managers have been thinking that something needs to be improved or changed but haven't felt comfortable about speaking up or simply haven't had time in the rush of doing everyday business. You need to give your managers a sense that you really want their opinions about your business: What are the opportunities? What are your strengths and weaknesses?

When reaching out to staff, make sure your internal-customer survey lets your employees express their opinions anonymously. These are the people who know the day-to-day business, who are the point of contact between your business and your customers, and you need their unfiltered advice. They can make or break you.

Many clients tell me at the start of this process, "The staff are just going to slam us." That's not always the case, but if they do, there might be an important lesson in it. The insights that come out of these surveys frequently surprise business owners and managers but that's not necessarily a bad thing.

We often hear managers complain to us, "My people aren't that bright," only to discover that they not only are bright, but caring and filled with valuable knowledge and insight.

The internal-customer survey must be self-administered, confidential, and anonymous. Your staff must not have any concern that one of them is going to be identified because she's writing with a blue pen and somebody else is writing with black and the boss is going to know who wrote which.

Put a staff member in charge of this process and hold an all-company meeting. Tell your staff why they're being asked to fill out the survey, that their feedback will be taken seriously, and that everything will be confidential and totally anonymous. To demonstrate that you mean what you say, have your employees drop their completed surveys into a preaddressed FedEx box that is sealed in their presence for shipping to a research company for tabulation.

Anonymity and confidentiality are important. Comments like "My manager is looking over my shoulder right now as I'm filling out this survey" are no help in formulating your Neighborhood Marketing program. It costs surprisingly little to have a research company administer the survey and tabulate the results, so don't cut corners and compromise your employees' confidence by trying to do it yourself. Show complete respect for their opinions and privacy. Build trust. What you'll get back is trustworthy employees.

In your internal survey, ask employees how they feel about themselves, how they feel about the company as an employer, what they think about the marketing. We often find that employees hate their uniforms, even the ones who get to wear a chic button-down black shirt and black pants. You may not want to change things, but you should know what they think before you go out and spend a fortune on your next set of uniforms.

Ask about their feelings on culture and diversity in the workplace. I'll address diversity marketing in more detail later, but do not underestimate the importance of this question. There are enormous and rapidly growing opportunities in marketing to customers with diverse backgrounds, and you ignore these at your peril. Again, social media can work for you or against you in this area. Your customers may feel you are either 'pro' diversity or 'anti' diversity and if the perception is negative it is very hard to change.

How do your employees feel about the salary and benefits you offer compared with other companies in the area? Of course they're going to think their salary and benefits are lower, but often this issue can be handled very simply. If you know they're misinformed, you can go out and do a little research yourself. If you're right, hold a staff meeting and show them in black and white that the grass is not really greener on the other side. You may, in this situation, even be able to reinforce some of the benefits you do offer, benefits your staff may not know about or understand.

If your employees are right, if their salaries and benefits are indeed on the low side, maybe you'll have a clue to high turnover, or low quality of staff performance, or any of a host of other issues. It all counts, and everything sells.

TYPICAL INTERNAL-CUSTOMER SURVEY QUESTIONS

(1 = I do not agree, 3 = somewhat agree, 5 = fully agree)

___ 1. I use my talents well at work; my skills and abilities are being fully utilized.

___ 2. I get along well with my supervisors.

___ 3. I am comfortable expressing my true feelings to others in a safe way.

___ 4. I view my employment here more as a career than as a job.

___ 5. There are things about working here that encourage me to work hard.

___ 6. There are work standards in place that enable me to judge my own job performance.

___ 7. Management is concerned with each individual co-worker's long-term goals.

___ 8. I look forward to going to work.

___ 9. I am asked for input when marketing programs are being evaluated; I feel I am an integral part of any marketing program.

___ 10. I am satisfied with my chances for getting ahead in this organization in the future.

___ 11. Would you recommend our business/establishment/service as a place to work?

___ 12. Would you recommend our business/establishment/service to your friends and family?

What Does It Mean?

What you do with the results of this survey is look inside the four walls of your business to see the big picture, and the many smaller pictures that make it up. These surveys should be broken down to give a total score for each store, if you have more than one outlet. Within the store, they should be broken down by category. In the food service business—the largest employer in America, with 12 million people working—you want results tabulated for back-of-the-house (kitchen staff), front-of-the-house (dining room and bar), and management.

In an auto dealership, you'd break it down by service (garage and service desk separately!), parts, sales (used and new), accounting, and so on. Be creative and look inside your four walls to see who your internal customers are, what categories they naturally fall into, and how they can be surveyed.

If you run a professional service business, such as an architecture firm, you've got a front-of-the-house in your receptionists; you've got back-of the-house internal customers in your design and drafting staff; you've got your sales executives, legal advisors, subcontractors, billing and accounting, and so on.

We often see these surveys produce fascinating and divergent results. You'd be surprised how many management surveys show zero percent recommending their own business as a place to either patronize or work. Guess where a business with that result needs to start in its marketing? If your managers hate your business, you need to figure out how to get them excited, engaged, or on their way to another job!

In a chef-driven restaurant, we often see that the back-of-the-house scores are better than the front. And if it's a business where there's a lot of customer contact and service, the scores in the front of the house will tend to be better.

Here's an important survey question, and the answer will be one of the most telling you get. Ask your employees if they see your business as a place they would recommend to friends or associates—either to patronize or to work. If your employees would not recommend you, you're missing a huge opportunity for improvement. Your staff, as your internal customers, should be among your most powerful marketing tools. (More about this later.)

Pay close attention to how likely your staff are to recommend your business as a place to work. If only one out of four employees does so, you need to address that before you start any external marketing program. Otherwise, you're wasting your efforts and driving customers to a bad experience, the opposite of the result you seek.

SURVEY YOUR CUSTOMERS

The surveys are beginning to pile up. And so is valuable, useful information coming out of your four walls, which will help you put together a winning Neighborhood Marketing plan.

The next area of information comes from your external Customer Attitude Profile Survey (CAPS).

In a busy retail operation, the survey should be done over several days to give you a representative sample of your customers. If you're in a retail business that's open seven days a week, do your survey on two weekdays and two weekend days. In companies that are busiest later in the week, the best days would be Thursday, Friday, Saturday, and Sunday. If you are in the food service business and you're open for lunch and dinner, it should be done at both times. If you're open breakfast, lunch, dinner, and late night, it should be done during each part of the day.

In any sort of retail business, your survey should be done during your busiest periods, without cutting corners or taking shortcuts. If you happen to be in a business that offers a product or service that is purchased with less spontaneity, the same idea applies, with some creativity.

The information you get from this survey is a demographic breakdown of your customers: age range, ethnicity, the number in a party (if your business is a restaurant), how often your customers patronize your business, whether they are male or female. It tells you who your target audience is. If you know who your customers are now, you know which part of your neighborhood to market to without shouting over the heads of people who aren't your prospects. It tells you statistically, not just what you think you know from seeing who is coming in the front door. You're looking for objective facts, not your intuition.

If you run a business that offers a frequency discount, how do you set the number of visits required? Start by determining your current customer frequency. This information is important, because it lets you craft a promotion that can impact your business very specifically and efficiently, instead of picking numbers out of the blue.

For best results, your promotion should be easy and accessible, so customers see the benefits sooner rather than later. Many business owners set the number too high, hoping to generate a large increase in sales. This is a mistake. If your survey shows you have a frequency per customer of 2.6 visits per month, you should set your frequency premium at 4 visits a month, which would increase your sales to these customers by up to 50 percent. The idea is not so much to increase sales immediately as to build loyalty—which, in turn, builds profits in the long term.

In general, I'm not a big fan of frequency programs unless they are structured well. Most people hate carrying those cards, don't remember them when they visit, and consider the whole thing an intrusion and a waste of time, so the benefit is often lost on them or, worse, becomes a turnoff. One option these days is to allow them their visits to be electronically tracked via their phone. Discounts can be scanned and points or credit given to each customer.

In food service, there are national databases that calculate the average national frequency of visits in each category. If the national casual dining average is 2.67 and your restaurant's frequency is lower, you know where you have room for improvement. This type of information makes the marketer's job easy.

In massaging this information, you should break down the frequency results into subcategories: what percent patronize once a month, twice a month, and so on. Suppose 10 percent of your customers visit your business four times a week. You want to nurture those customers, of course, but they are already loyal and above-average visitors without any incentive.

Suppose 15 percent visit once a week. What would happen to your business if you could move them up to the next category, two to three visits a week, or even four? That would have a huge impact on sales. Detailed research, properly conducted, tells you exactly where to focus your efforts and spend your dollars for greatest profitability.

The Customer Attitude Profile Survey also collects information on guest satisfaction. How many rate you excellent on product quality? Service? Hospitality? Atmosphere? Value?

Here is one of the most important pieces of data you will get: how do your customers rate you versus your competitors? It may reassure you and stroke your ego to know that they say you're great on your own, but often those results conflict with what customers say when they rate you against the competition.

If only 25 percent rate your business better than your competitors on quality and service, that means three out of four of your customers think you're the same or worse. This tells you you're lacking a competitive edge—that when your customers have four places to choose from, there isn't really much that's distinguishing you. You aren't wowing them. You are unremarkable and therefore invisible.

Interviewing customers is something many business owners and managers hate doing. They respect their customers' privacy, or they may be afraid to hear bad news, or they may be uncomfortable having that sort of conversation with people.

Get over it. Customers love to talk about themselves and their experiences. You can use a email, electronic or even a print card with 20 questions on it and a simple check off system, with ratings from best to worst. That often works well in busy places, as long as your employees are trained to encourage customers to fill them out.

Customers who frequent upscale businesses prefer to be interviewed. Make sure you train interviewers well about exactly how you want the survey done. You can hire interviewers, but be aware that the people consultants hire for these positions often aren't top quality and may know little about your business.

Be that as it may, there is little statistical difference between having somebody interview customers and asking customers to fill out cards. Somebody in the business should be assigned to distribute survey cards to customers, with specific instructions on how to collect them. It's useful to train one person for that responsibility. To avoid skewing the results, assign someone who doesn't usually have contact with your customers to distribute cards or conduct interviews.

You shouldn't be surprised to learn that customers are eager to give their opinion – especially since they have been conditioned to tweet or share that opinion with the universe at a moment's notice. They want to tell you what's going on and are often offended if they see that you're running a survey that they haven't been invited to participate in.

Always conduct your survey after customers have had their experience. Let them know that you're doing a survey and ask them politely if they will fill out the form or answer the questions. Select attractive young men and women with good people skills to collect your data. Be sure you design a survey or an interview that takes no more than three minutes to complete.

Identify where your customers come from. A nifty device to identify your principal trading area—your neighborhood—is a dot map. You can use an electronic map of your area and overlay dots to represent customers. If you're measuring different parts of the day, use a different overlay for each part. Project it on a screen or monitor in your lobby. As customers arrive, ask each one where he was just before coming to your store, and attach a dot to that location. Then ask the customer where he lives, and mark that location with a dot of a different color.

This is simple, it's enormously valuable, and customers get a kick out of it. They love maps, they love seeing where everyone else comes from, and they love to be asked about themselves.

Make sure your employees understand how important this is and how it works. We once had a client bring in his printed map. His employees were proud that they had followed the instructions—but instead of putting the dots on the map locations, they had arranged them in the shape of a smiley face.

When you're done, you'll have a clear picture of your principal trading area. If you use different overlays for different parts of the day, week, or month, you may begin to see certain patterns: your business in the morning may be drawing from the commuters heading south on the main road, but on the weekends from your backyard. Armed with this information, you know exactly where to spend your marketing time and dollars. The dot-map exercise should take place for a seven-day period.

BACK-OFFICE DATA

At least once a year, take your spreadsheets and other bookkeeping data and plot them on graphs. Look at the trends. I recommend plotting a three year trend. If you do only two years, the results may be skewed by unusual events in your market—a blizzard, road construction, or some other extraneous factor over which you have no control. Three years is harder to distort, and it helps you see the predictable peaks and valleys for scheduling your promotions. You may think you know when those peaks are, and you might be right. But more often than not, business managers find hidden surprises in these charts.

The mountain of infomation—and of valuable knowledge—is growing. You are getting deeper inside your four walls.

Break your sales down as much as you can: by part of the day, transaction size, weekday versus weekend, product or service, and so on. This will show where you're hurting and where you need a boost. Later, it will also help you measure how successful you were in meeting your marketing goals.

Look at your product or service mix. What are your best sellers? Which contribute the highest profit? If you're going to do a promotion to attract new customers, the best thing to promote would be your most popular product or service. Your existing customers already like it, so new customers will probably like it as well and are more likely to become repeaters.

What is the most profitable product? When you design staff incentives, you want to encourage them to sell your most profitable items or services. They may tend to sell the item that increases the ticket the most but on which you hardly make any money.

SHOP THE COMPETITION

Check out your competition. Too many businesspeople neglect to do this. How in the world will you know where you stand in your market and your category if you don't keep a weather eye on the other guy?

Do competitive shopping, but go with an open mind. Don't waste a lot of time looking for what your competitors are doing wrong. We all tend to do this; it makes us feel better, superior, and helps confirm that what we are doing is right. But finding an excuse to congratulate yourself is not the objective.

Here's a better idea. Send your employees out to do your competitive shopping. Have them come back with 10 things the other guys are doing right. Think about that. What could you possibly learn from paying attention to what your competitor is doing wrong? What you really want to know is why those customers are in the other guy's store instead of yours.

Are you in the carpet business? Send your salespeople to other showrooms to comparison shop. Or have them call for an in-home estimate from all your competitors. Don't ask a friend or family member. Make sure your employees are learning firsthand what tricks the competition has up its sleeve.

Are you in the plumbing business? Have your plumbers call other plumbers to come in and give an estimate to replace a toilet or perform some other service. Be creative. Have your staff study every aspect of the other guy's business, from how he answers the telephone to how he prices his product or service. Your employees will come back with ideas they can incorporate into their work.

Once you've allowed your employees to discover ways they can improve customer service and grow your business, you've recruited them to your own cause. You've given them respect and dignity. You've made them, in effect, your partners. They've become your loyal internal customers—which they would not be if you had simply gone out yourself and come back to bestow your newfound wisdom on them.

Don't do this once and forget about it. Make it a regular program. Send your staff out once a month or once a quarter, whichever is appropriate to your business. Have them use Forms B1 through B3 either in print form or you can create an electronic version.

KEEPING TRACK

How many times have you said to yourself, "I need to do a promotion, but I can't remember the details of the one we did last year that worked so well"? Here's how to avoid that pothole: Keep records of every marketing promotion you ever run, along with a close analysis, cost sheet, and a copy of the promotional piece or other materials.

Yes, it's a pain. By the time a promotion is over you're sick of it and ready for a break. But nothing tells you what works better than what worked well. We tend to want a cool, new idea, something that'll get us excited. Instead, you could take an old idea that worked well and tweak it, and do it again. You may be bored with it, but your customers may not be. Sometimes the same promotion at the same time of year works better than the cool new idea. What's the goal, to increase your sales or fix your boredom?

In looking back at previous promotions, make sure to record and take into account factors that might have skewed the result, such as interruptions in business from weather. Maybe the staff didn't like it. Was it confusing? Capture that information when you're running the promotion and right after it's over. If you wait, you'll forget.

DON'T GAG—SPIT ON THE COMPETITION

Remember the seven steps, and make sure you do them all.

G = Gathering data

A = Analyzing data

G = Goal setting

If you stop here, your business will GAG on your promotional efforts.

Keep going and you'll SPIT on the competition.

S = Strategy developing

P = Planning

I = Implementing

T = Tracking and evaluating

CHAPTER 4

READ THE TEA LEAVES

*The greatest thing in this world is not so much where
we are, but in what direction we are moving.*

OLIVER WENDELL HOLMES,
UNITED STATES SUPREME COURT JUSTICE

CHAPTER 4

THE AMERICAN PSYCHOLOGIST AND AUTHOR Alfred J. Marrow once conducted an experiment in goal-setting at a clothing factory he operated in Virginia. He was trying to figure out how to fashion a system that would motivate new employees to reach certain performance standards.

Marrow took a group of new, unskilled employees, set a production quota that was hard to achieve, and gave them three months to meet it. At the end, the group had missed the mark by about one-third.

He then took a second group, also unskilled, and set progressive goals, raising the bar a little each week. As the workers' proficiency increased, the goals were raised. At the end of the same period, the group had met the ultimate goal.

Every business operator should attack each of his or her goals with the same measured approach. Home runs are great, but the game is really won by singles and doubles, good fielding and relentless pitching, inning by inning.

You've gathered your data in step one in the previous chapter. Now it's time to read the tea leaves and start setting realistic, motivating goals and objectives.

STEP 2: ANALYZE YOUR DATA

Once you've gathered all your external- and internal-customer information and other business data, you need to sit down and figure out how to read the clues. You want to identify clear strengths and weaknesses. Weaknesses must be addressed. Strengths should be built on.

If your customer attitude profile shows excellent product ratings but poor service, you've got work to do with your internal customers. Now you look at your internal-customer attitude; perhaps it shows your staff has excellent self-esteem but lacks training. The first step in your marketing plan is to put together a more effective training program.

Look at each piece of data. Gather all your paperwork and set aside some quiet time, free of distraction. Get a red pen and a green pen; use the green pen to circle or highlight strengths and the red one for weaknesses. This is another chance for you to visualize your business. You are going still deeper inside your four walls.

PRIORITIZE YOUR STRENGTHS AND WEAKNESSES

After you've circled your strengths and weaknesses, you've got to prioritize them. You may identify 20 strengths and 20 weaknesses, but you won't be able to tackle them all. Which are the most important? Which is the one that can have the most immediate impact? Which is the one that is most achievable?

We once ran a marketing boot camp for a chain of stores in which we asked a group of employees, after going through an in-depth data analysis, to pick their top weakness. One store manager stood up and declared, "My greatest weakness is I need a bigger office." The owner of the company, who was sitting in back, let out a low groan. This woman was, as they say, unclear on the concept. The first item in that company's marketing plan should have been her rapid replacement.

Clients often complete this process, become overwhelmed, and feel there's nothing they can do about some of their problems. For example, in the retail industry there's a lot of anguish over local zoning and signage laws. If your problem is that the city won't let you put a banner on the front of your store, is the solution to try to change the law? Be practical, and creative!

A Subway franchise facing this issue in Arizona made up a bunch of folding window shades that people put on their dashboards when they park. On one side was the Subway logo. They gave one to every employee and had them park their cars facing the street and put the shades in their windows. There's no law against window shades, at least not yet!

Ask yourself: What are my top three issues? That's as many as you can focus on at once. Take care of those, then move on to the next three, and so on. By the inch it's a cinch. By the yard it's hard.

Marketing Conclusions

Out of all this information and data, you now develop a marketing conclusion. Restate the strengths and weaknesses you circled. Did you find excellent ratings for product quality but low marks on service? Employees have high self-esteem but don't get effective training? You need to fix your training program so your internal customers can contribute to your Neighborhood Marketing plan.

Be SMAART:

S = Specific. "Improving service" is not specific. How, exactly, will you improve it?

M = Measurable. Will you be able to tell how well you are meeting your goals?

A = Aggressive. Many people don't set stretch goals. Identify what you think you can do comfortably, then move the bar a little higher. Ask yourself, What is possible if we get cranking?

A = Accountable. Who's in charge? Who is responsible for making it all come together?

R = Realistic. Nothing kills enthusiasm faster than impossible goals.

T = Time-Specific. Goals need to be achieved by a certain date or within a certain period.

Keep funneling your information down, narrowing your analysis more and more, until you can state the case in simple terms.

Here's a sample conclusion: Customer attitude ratings were poor for service; therefore, marketing efforts will focus on training staff in the fundamentals and finer points of service and hospitality, as well as on measuring and rewarding great service in the store.

Step 3: Set Goals and Objectives

You may have read to this point and be mentally exhausted and ready for some fun tactics and promotions. But first, you need to define your objectives based on what your research has told you.

Setting goals and objectives is crucial to an efficient, successful Neighborhood Marketing plan.

Look at your objectives with creativity. Financial objectives are SMAART, and they're easy to identify. But nonfinancial objectives, such as increasing your customer attitude profile scores and lowering employee turnover, are also SMAART. They're specific, measurable, aggressive, accountable, realistic, and potentially time-specific.

STEP 4. DEVELOP A STRATEGY

There are many ways to increase sales, many different kinds of promotions you can create and execute. As a manager or owner, you are responsible for choosing or designing the promotions that will best accomplish your SMAART objectives.

You're eager to get to the fun part, the hands-on stuff, aren't you? Yes, I'm talking about tactics. Everybody likes playing around with tactics, and you're sorely tempted to skip the rest of the planning process and get on with the fun.

Resist the temptation. Before you sketch out your tactics, you've got to do some clear thinking about what it will take to achieve your objectives. That is, you have to design your strategy.

Suppose one of your SMAART objectives is to increase sales between September 1 and December 31, and you've come up with two possible strategies. One is to target office workers in your trading area. Another is to build sales by targeting tourists. If you target both of these audiences, will that lead to your objective in the most effective and direct manner?

How many different ways can a restaurant promote itself to office workers? You can do a business blitz, taking samples of food and menus to area offices. You can launch an office-runner program, offering a free meal to the runner who comes in and picks up an office order over a certain amount. There are dozens of tactics to consider.

In a tourist-related market, you can implement a concierge program with local hotels. You can market to cab drivers so they know where you are.

Every retail business is besieged with requests for donations to local nonprofit groups. When you get sick enough of saying no, how about taking charge of the situation? Choose the fundraising organization that you want to associate with and do a promotion with them that as an added benefit will bring traffic to your business.

Think ahead. Identify the list of possible tactics and target audiences, prioritize them, then go after them.

Focus your efforts. More isn't always better. It's more effective to do a couple of programs well than to have 20 different programs limping along simultaneously.

As you identify each target audience in your area, ask yourself what general action you're going to take, and what is the desired result.

TACTICS

Many businesspeople make the mistake of putting this step ahead of all the others. It's important to build your plan based on the knowledge you've gained to this point, and an assessment of what you can actually accomplish.

At a marketing boot camp we recently ran, a participant came up with a single tactic for his objective. We pointed out that this was a little risky, putting all his eggs in one basket. He agreed, but when he went back to the drawing board, instead of developing other tactics, he lowered his objective. That's not how it works.

In developing your tactics, you need to put them on a calendar to make sure you don't have too much going on at the same time. This is yet another visual tool to help you see inside your four walls.

Businesses often make the mistake of forgetting to do this, then suddenly find they've scheduled five events or promotions for the same month. If you do this, you won't know which had the greatest impact on your sales and which didn't work. You're going to have way too many things going on. Your customers will be confused, your internal customers exhausted, and your business chaotic.

What's the solution? It may be as simple as rescheduling one event, or as complicated as rethinking your whole Neighborhood Marketing plan. Ask yourself, instead of a one-year plan, am I really writing a two-year plan? If you've come up with a lot of great ideas, consider spreading them out.

In developing your tactics, factor into everything the labor you'll need, the promotional materials, and your marketing investment as a percentage of sales. A good rule of thumb is to spend 3 to 4 percent of your gross sales.

Training should be part of your marketing budget. Human resources will love you, because their training budgets are usually tight. You shouldn't mind, because seeing training as a marketing function and investment gets you closer to, and gives you more control over, the results you seek. I'd rather see a business spend marketing money for training than yet another advertising insert or coupon promotion. Training will have more of an impact on sales. Companies that focus their efforts on training, such as Starbucks, Disney, Federal Express, and The Cheesecake Factory, consistently outperform companies that divert more of their resources into advertising.

STEP 5. IMPLEMENT THE PLAN

This step is covered in a later chapter on promotional tactics and how to put them into play.

STEP 6. TRACK PROGRESS

Stay on top of your marketing promotion as it happens. Without proper supervision and attention, a terrific start can quickly bog down. On Day 1, everyone's on board and paying attention. Day 2, if you aren't tracking how it's going, people get distracted and fall back into old patterns. Don't squander your promotion by assuming that once you've set everything up and pulled the trigger, it's all going to come off like clockwork. You may need to tweak, remind, cajole, encourage, and otherwise shepherd it through its successful completion. Take the pulse regularly and correct any misunderstandings or missteps. Support your managers and staff.

STEP 7: EVALUATE THE RESULT

How did it go? Look at how you did both quantitatively and qualitatively. What did your customers think? What did your employees think? Was it easy or hard to implement? What other intangibles affected the success of the promotion? What was the weather like?

For the number crunching, don't fall into the common trap of looking only at top-line sales. Most people just tally up the coupon redemptions and start thinking about the next promotion.

Take some time and look at the growth-rate impact factor. Look at your promotion in context to get a true picture of how you did. If you ran a marketing promotion that lasted a month, look at the sales trends for the months before and after. My clients are often surprised to learn that the sales increase they experienced is temporary and that they are actually addicting their customers to coupons or discounts.

Here's an example for a one-month promotion. Compare this April with last April. At first glance, you hit it out of the ballpark: up 10 percent. Your number of transactions was up, and so was your average ticket.

Now look at March, the month before the promotion. Sales were up 4 percent over the prior year. Looks like you had a 6 percent net gain, all other factors being equal. Not bad, but not quite over the fence.

What if your sales were flat during a promotion? A disaster? Maybe, maybe not. One of our clients, a 35-unit chain, saw sales rise only 1.8 percent during a promotion. They thought it hadn't worked. But when we looked back two years, we discovered that they were down 10 percent. So the promotion actually yielded an 11.8 percent bump: out of the ballpark.

Another example: suppose sales during the promotion are up 10 percent over the previous year, but when you look at the sales in May, the month after, they're up only 8 percent. You lost 2 percent of the sales you gained during the promotion, right? Not necessarily. You drill deeper into the numbers and discover that sales in March were up 4 percent over the year before. You can fairly say that the promotion brought in 4 percent more revenue.

That's how you stair-step and build your business. If you're not holding onto the residual after your promotion, you may be doing too many promotions, the wrong ones at the wrong time, the right ones at the wrong time—or even the right ones at the right time, but with the wrong internal customers. The permutations are endless. Did a new competitor open that month? What was the weather like? How was the economy? What did guests say in your customer surveys? How easy was it to execute? What did management say? What did your staff say?

Record all of this so next time you can build on what you've learned. You will find more detailed information in Chapter 24. Forms for measuring promotion performance are available in the appendices and on our Web site, www.tomfeltenstein.com.

CHAPTER 5

ADVENTURES IN PROMOTION

*Neighborhood Marketing builds brands over time in
each trading area and sales overnight.*

TOM FELTENSTEIN

CHAPTER 5

BY NOW YOU SHOULD BE ALL REVVED UP and ready to conquer the world. There's much more to know about how to implement the Neighborhood Marketing plan you just wrote: how to find and keep great employees, how to write your promotional materials so they get the biggest result, social media marketing, diversity marketing, direct mail, and much more.

But you want some great ideas, so here are a few to get you going.

GET AGGRESSIVE

The owner of a chain of three pizza shops in West Palm Beach, Florida, had a good, solid, growing business until Domino's rode into town. In no time he found himself looking out his window and shaking his head in dismay as a caravan of Domino's delivery cars rolled past all day long. When he opened his first pizza shop, years earlier, few people had never heard of Domino's.

His business was still good, but growth had stalled. He specialized in delivery, but now he was being squeezed out of his own market. He'd wasted a lot of hard-earned and even borrowed money on TV commercials, billboards, radio spots, and running ads in the local papers. None of it moved the needle.

When I met this entrepreneur, he was about as frustrated as any businessperson I've met. "I don't get it. I used mass marketing for the past 15 years and it worked. It's not working for me now, and Domino's has 40 stores in my market."

I suggested he hire people to go door-to-door and march the streets spreading this message: "Cut the Domino's ad out of your Yellow Pages and bring it in for 25 percent off any pizza." He put up posters promoting the campaign in his three stores, inside his four walls. We had all of his employees wear buttons that said, "Ask me about the Yellow Pages."

And they did. The campaign, a real David versus Goliath gambit, generated excitement and provided weeks of word-of-mouth marketing. His sales took off, and so did repeat business! As a side benefit, hundreds of phone books lost their Domino's ads.

CALL UP THE MARINES

Even the Marine Corps has benefited from Neighborhood Marketing. Former McDonald's CEO Ed Rensi is now head of his own competitive auto racing company, Rensi Motor Sports Racing Team. As an ex-Marine, he wanted to see if he could help the Marine Corps in its recruiting efforts. He recently spoke at one of my marketing conferences, describing how he did it.

The United States Marine Corps, formed 230 years ago, is an institution that has remained true to its values. They have three primary missions: recruit young men and women who are capable of being Marines; win battles; and return those young men and women back to the civilian corps as better citizens.

To do this they have to recruit 43,000 new Marines a year. Mom is an instant disqualifier. Johnny comes home from school and says, "I talked to a Marine Corps recruiter today and I want to join the Marine Corps." Mom grabs her heart, falls back in her chair, and says, "How can you do this to me?"

The Marine Corps recognizes how important Mom and the parents are in the decision-making process. So at a race in New Hampshire one Mother's Day, we wanted to make a statement to potential Marine Corps families. We bought 40,000 red carnations and had about 40 Marines in their crisp, full-dress uniforms come to the racetrack and stand in front of the entrance gates.

"Every woman who walked into the stadium who looked like she might be a mother was presented with a carnation. The Marine who handed her the carnation came to attention, gave her a smart salute, and said, "The Marine Corps wishes you a Happy Mother's Day."

On the car we had entered in the race that day we painted "Happy Mother's Day, Mom, United States Marine Corps."

For that $4,000 expenditure for carnations we generated almost $3 million of media coverage from the New York border into New England. That wasn't a mass media buy, that was Neighborhood Marketing. That was saying to our neighborhood guests, "We value you as a member of our team. We care about you as an individual." We generated more than $2 million worth of radio and television air time. A total of $5 million of marketing value was created for an outlay of $4,000. The goodwill generated was immeasurable.

Protest Yourself

Picket your own store. Make signs proclaiming the positive points of your business and have your employees or specially hired help walk the few blocks around your store. Take pictures and video to share on your social media sites. We did this with a store in South Florida and it stirred up an incredible amount of attention and enthusiasm in the neighborhood. So many people were tickled to see "positive picketing" that reporters and news crews, including CNN, showed up to investigate the ruckus. Sales jumped that month and stayed above the store's average sales prior to the campaign. This is one of those visual promotions that was MADE for social media. Videos, updates to Twitter and Facebook will keep help it go viral and really get some attention!

Join the Club

Create a VIP Club. Invite your regular customers to join. You know who they are. Give them a VIP card, priority service, membership-only invitations to sales, special parking spaces, and other perks. To build awareness of the club and its rewards, conduct the initial membership drive within your four walls with posters and displays and via social media.

Train your cashiers to ask customers if they are members of the VIP Club. If not, encourage them to join. Membership is free, and all the customer need do is fill out a data capture card: name, mailing address, e-mail address, phone number, birthday, anniversary, and any other information that you can put to future marketing use such as "Like us on Facebook for a free desert!"

The less information customers have to provide, the more likely they'll take time to join. Make sure the questions you're asking support your business objectives, and that the perks are valuable to your customers.

"Data capture" is a fancy term for obtaining your guests' personal information: name, street address, e-mail address, phone number, birthday, anniversary—anything they're willing to provide. Getting this information lets you motivate, excite, and bond with them by sending them personalized messages every couple of months about products or services that might interest them. Offer Maggie a free, three-pound lobster on her birthday, and you're likely to sell her dinner for four to go with it. A discounted sapphire bracelet might interest Maggie's husband Joe on their eighth wedding anniversary. Make your customers feel as though you're looking out for their interests. Let your imagination be your guide.

JACKPOT

If your business is located in a state that has a lottery, give away tickets to increase visit frequency and interest in special sales. When the jackpot reaches $20 million, buy $100 worth of lottery tickets and hand out one with each purchase of the item or service that you're promoting. Instruct your sales team or servers to call customers' attention to the potential for a major payday. Hang promotional posters in highly visible areas to entice customer involvement and share on social media to create online excitement. Once the posters are created, you can repeat the promotion every time the lottery jackpot swells.

HAVE A BALL

Here's a graphic illustration of the power of neighborhood thinking, and proof of my argument that targeted marketing within a 10-minute drive of your front door is your best approach. A few years ago, I designed a campaign for a store in Huntsville, Alabama. We bought 5,000 bright yellow Ping-Pong balls and printed prizes on them, along with the name of the store. We rented a helicopter and dropped the balls over a 20-mile radius on one side of town.

On the other side of town, we sent out 5,000 direct-mail pieces to people living within a three-mile radius of the store. The direct-mail pieces offered the same prizes that were printed on the Ping-Pong balls. We had a 20 percent same-store sales increase from the direct-mail pieces. We got only a 2 percent increase where the balls were scattered.

Why does mass marketing fail? Because it's like aiming at a target while blindfolded. Given unlimited ammunition (or enough Ping-Pong balls), you'll eventually hit the target, but look at all the bullets you'll waste.

EYE-CATCHERS

Think about creating colorful, interactive, dazzling displays to promote your products in every zone of your business—at the front counter, in the waiting or reception area, in the service or product area, even in the parking lot. Every zone represents an opportunity to remind your customers how much they should appreciate your outstanding products and services and your proximity to their workplaces and homes.

Place colorful posters in your restroom stalls promoting your products and services. If you own a restaurant, create a dessert sampler to entice diners to try your sweets, and display it prominently near the entrance or in the dining room. If you own an office supply store, make up a sample travel kit—everything a businessperson needs while on the go—and display it prominently.

Instead of counting on a three-second glimpse of a billboard in heavy traffic or 30 seconds on a television screen, put yourself on display constantly, each and every moment your customers are within or immediately outside the four walls of your business and every moment they spend on social media.

GOOD FORTUNE

Instead of buying a scattershot newspaper ad offering the world a discount on your products or services, reward the customers you already have with fortune cookies containing promotional premiums, such as a percentage off their purchase. When it's time to pay, customers pick a fortune cookie out of a bowl, break it open, and get their reward. One clothing store let customers select their fortune cookie when they entered the store and discover their discount (from 5 to 20 percent, they were told) upfront. Those whose cookies contained a 20 percent discount "fortune" wanted to buy as much as possible to take advantage of the deal. The most interesting aspect of the promotion: most of the cookies gave shoppers 20 percent off. The promotion boosted the average ticket by about 10 percent and raised gross profits by 1 percent.

You can even use fortune cookies as part of a direct-mail campaign. A pharmaceutical company that wanted to tell doctors about a new medication did a direct mailing that had a message inside a fortune cookie, which was packed inside a traditional Chinese food carry-out container, which was packed inside a white corrugated shipping box. The program had three mailings, a week apart, with the product information included as an insert in the shipping box. The response rate averaged a whopping 25 percent. (For information on ordering specialty fortune cookies, see References in Appendix B.)

ABOVE AND BEYOND

You probably don't own an airline, but you've flown and have suffered the many indignities they heap on customers these days. That's why I have to tell you about the time I was actually surprised and delighted by an airline. Because I travel a lot, I'm a Platinum flier, although it doesn't get me much in the way of perks.

I got off a plane in Atlanta, and two Delta gate staffers stopped me to tell me they appreciated my flying Delta. They asked, "Are you staying over?"

"As a matter of fact, I am," I replied.

"We would like to surprise and delight you."

I said I hadn't been delighted in 10 years.

"We have some tickets to an Atlanta Braves game that we would like to give you if you'd like to go."

I was stunned. They had no idea I was a frequent flier, either. They presented me the tickets in an envelope that had "Surprise" and "Delight" printed on it.

SMILE BUTTON

It's sometimes hard to get your sales staff to smile, but here's something that will make it worth their while and generate a lot of hospitality: the two-dollar smile button. Buy some cheap smiley-face buttons and attach to them a $2 bill (it's unusual and interesting on its own) with a little sign that says, "If I don't smile, you get this $2 bill."

Give your staff members one $2 bill each day, and tell them they can keep the ones they don't have to give away. That'll keep them grinning!

READ AND RELAX

Independent bookstores have been battered in recent years by huge bookstore chains and Amazon.com. Yet they can survive, and even thrive, by aggressively marketing to their neighborhoods. Do what the big stores do. Put in some comfortable couches. Have an information counter right at the front door and keep it staffed at all times. Bookstore customers get frustrated quickly when they can't find what they're looking for.

Have a host or server go around to people who are sitting and reading and offer to bring them a cup of coffee or a sandwich.

HIDDEN GOLD

Banks are among the worst at Neighborhood Marketing. This makes no sense at all, because banks do most of their business in their own neighborhoods. They spend millions on advertising, but I have yet to see a single bank ad that didn't make the same tired claim: "Your Friendly Neighborhood Bank."

The two banks that I do business with have never once asked me what I need. You'd think they'd come visit me and say, "Look, you're a really great customer. Here are the five services you use. Here are 20 more we'd like to tell you about. We would like to do more for you. We know you have money set aside in a money-market fund. Why don't you let our trust department set up a trust account for your kids?"

They've got all these products, they know just about everything about me, they know where I live, what I spend, what I save. They've got a built-in market to sell the other products. It amazes me that they don't mine the gold they already have inside their four walls. Most customers are worth much more to a bank, despite the way they are often treated.

Okay, let's get back to work and find out how to hire and keep great employees.

HOW TO LOSE YOUR BEST CUSTOMER

An old man walked into a bank. There were seven teller windows; two were open, the other five closed. To get to a teller window, customers had to negotiate a Disney-like maze of ropes.

The old man waited patiently. He tried to fill out a transaction slip, but the pen was on a chain and the chain happened to be just a little too short to let him write comfortably. He asked one of the tellers: "Why the chains?"

"People take the pens," said the teller.

"So what?" said the old man, and he ripped the pen off the chain.

Finally, another teller returned from a two-hour lunch, slowly opened up his window and asked the old man to approach.

The old man asked, "Will you validate my parking?"

"You have to make a transaction before I can validate your parking."

"Okay," said the old man. "I'll give you a transaction—close my accounts."

It turns out that the old man had more than a million dollars in various accounts at that bank. The bank could have kept his business. All they had to do was be hospitable and know their customer.

CHAPTER 6

HIRE EAGLES NOT TURKEYS

Eagles don't flock. You have to find them one at a time.

H. ROSS PEROT

CHAPTER 6

TO TAKE A MARKETING APPROACH, you should always be looking for your next employee. If you only recruit when you have a job opening, you can't get the best. You should recruit new employees the same way you market to attract new customers—proactively and consistently. All recruiting is advertising; all advertising is recruiting.

I once wandered into an ice-cream store in the Bronx, New York City, that was like any other ice-cream shop you'll find anywhere except for a couple of obvious differences. It was sparkling clean and it was a lot better run. The employees were helpful, smiling, and eager to please.

Sitting prominently on the counter was a stack of the owner's business cards. In addition to all the usual information, the card said, "If you have any comments at all about my store, please call me at home," and gave the owner's home phone number.

You couldn't help noticing the cards.

The owner's internal customers, his employees, couldn't help noticing the walk-in customers eyeballing those cards and pocketing them.

It's all about accountability. The rest is human nature.

MANAGE TURNOVER

New clients often expect me to start talking about product differentiation and how to advertise with snappy slogans. I sometimes surprise a client when I start a marketing discussion by talking about the quality of their internal customers. And I always hear the same tired responses: "You can't get good help." "Nobody cares about customer service anymore." "I can't afford to hire the good people." "These kids today. . . ." On and on.

Business owners complain that we have a recruiting problem in America, but they're dead wrong about that. What we have is a retention problem, because our hiring processes and decisions are terrible and we don't take care of who we employ.

Red Auerbach, the legendary coach of the Boston Celtics basketball team, once said, "If you hire the wrong people, all the fancy management tactics in the world won't help you out." You should develop a profile of who you want to be a member of your staff. If you do that, the rest is easy. Low-cost employees are expensive if they quit in three months—and the most expensive person you hire is the person you have to fire.

Turnover is the biggest problem with staffing. Your goal should be not to eliminate turnover but to manage it.

Employee turnover is costly beyond belief. On average, the cost for turning over a single manager averages about $26,000 per year (it ranges from $22,000 to $30,000). If you have a large organization and you turn over 100 managers in a year—this is a cost of $2.6 million to the company. Does it not make sense then to hire only the very best? And once they are representing you in your own four walls, does it not pay to train them, keep them, and promote them? Make the work experience, the pay, and the job satisfaction so outrageous they never think of leaving. One of the most neglected aspects of all businesses that I've worked with is the internal customers, and it is the fulcrum of all marketing.

I know it's hard to find eagles in the huge flock of turkeys out there looking for "a job," because so many of the turkeys have learned to dress up like eagles. So we hire them, thinking they're eagles, and when they start acting like the turkeys they are, we figure it's a training problem. When more training doesn't help, we figure it's a motivational problem, so we institute a motivational program. But if that eagle really is a turkey, things don't improve, and we end up with a trained, motivated turkey.

On the other hand, poorly trained eagles can make you think they're turkeys. If you've got people who don't seem up to the job but keep asking for training, you may be looking at eagles in turkey outfits. The real turkeys are the ones who don't ask for training but are content to just gobble along.

You can't train people to be sunshine. Everyone likes to learn, but no one wants to be trained. They resent it because it's just like school, which isn't really about learning but short-term memorization.

Your frontline is your bottom line. They have to smile. That's the number one ingredient. Suppose you find someone who doesn't smile but seems awesome in every other respect. You think, I can teach this person to smile. You're wrong. If you can't use this person in a position that doesn't require customer contact, you should wish her good luck on her continued job search.

You must determine upfront exactly what qualities you want in your employees. You want people who are experienced, people who already have a job and are good at it.

RECRUIT 24/7

Your first assignment is to get some cards that say, "You were really terrific. If you're ever looking for another job, please give me a call," and give your phone number and your business name. The next time you encounter great customer service and think, I wish my employees were like that, hand that person one of these cards. You should always be recruiting, even when you don't need anyone—because sooner or later, you will.

One of the best places to recruit is from your competitors. Visit the other businesses in your category and neighborhood. Study their staff, and when you see someone you wish was working for you, give her one of your cards.

Many years ago, the manager of a small-town hotel was sitting quietly at the front desk late one night when a couple arrived. They seemed tired and bitter; he assumed it was due to the bad weather. The gentleman, a man of some stature, perhaps in his mid-50s, approached the desk and asked the manager for a room. The manager replied, "Sir, due to the harsh conditions outside, we are filled to the brim! Let me see if one of our suites is available." He checked, but there was not a single room available in the entire hotel. The gentleman glanced at his wife and let out a sigh.

The manager stood up and said, "Sir, I can't find a room to rent you, but I can see that you are tired and in need of some rest. Please take my room for the evening, and make yourselves comfortable." Without waiting for a reply, the manager picked up the couple's luggage and led them to his own modest but well-kept room.

As the manager turned to leave, the gentleman stopped him. "You know," he said, "one day I am going to call you, and you will become the manager at my hotel." The manager nodded politely and left.

A few months later, the manager received a phone call from the gentleman, asking if he would be interested in moving to New York. The gentleman, it turns out, was the owner of the greatest hotel in New York City—and now, by virtue of his superb hospitality, the former manager of the small hotel is the manager at the Waldorf-Astoria.

Remember those Wal-Mart TV ads showing a mother persuading her daughter with two degrees that Wal-Mart is a great place to work? Wal-Mart employs about 1.4 million people, more than General Motors. Each year it hires 600,000 new people. Which is a more effective way for Wal-Mart to recruit, through tiny generic classified ads, or by sending out a warm and fuzzy message that "we are family"?

I invited a number of businesspeople who have been successful at recruiting and retaining employees to one of my recent marketing conferences. Here are a few lessons that have been learned and that you can adapt to your business.

PERSON TO PERSON

Blimpie stays clear of the mass media approach to attracting employees. The company figured out that it makes no sense to put an advertisement in the newspaper and attract 50 applicants when only 2 are needed, then have to spend three days telling 48 of them they aren't needed.

Blimpie recruits through the hundreds of customers coming into their store. When the manager spots someone with great people skills, she asks, "You wouldn't have any friends or family members who need a job, would you?"

It works. The store quickly finds the people it needs. Customers feel complimented. The manager is credited with having the judgment to identify the customer as somebody with good personal qualities. The person who is asked is either personally interested in the job or knows other people with similar qualities.

Blimpie also recruits within its four walls and neighborhood by offering current employees a $100 bonus for recruiting someone else.

Blimpie has a fairly simple business operation, and the hurdle to employment with the company is simple as well. Applicants are tested for basic math skills and then asked what they would do if a customer told them that a sandwich was rotten. Their answer always reveals whether they have the innate ability to think clearly and whether they are naturally good at caring about people.

COUNTER CULTURE

Hard Rock Café, a chain of youth-music-oriented restaurants and clubs, likes applicants who show up dressed strangely. Its employment ads are edgy and provocative, with titles like "Not working here must really suck." That particular ad won a marketing award.

The company places ads in free, alternative urban newspapers that cover the music scene and are read by its "Generation Y" target audience. It offers a $50 bounty to any employee who brings someone aboard who stays more than 90 days.

BEHAVIOR-BASED

June Thompson, of the Atlanta Marriott organization, reports that her company does quite a bit of hiring on college campuses and offers mentorships and internships through local high schools. Job shadowing and mentoring give young people a taste of what hospitality is all about and a chance to see if they are a good fit in the hospitality industry.

Marriott also practices behavioral interviewing. June reports, "We used to ask applicants to tell us about their strengths, accomplishments, and weaknesses. But we learned that most people have prepared answers."

Now Marriott's interviewers say, "Tell me about the time you had to deal with a difficult customer and the outcome was good (or not good), what steps you took to resolve the situation, and who else in your workplace you involved." With that question alone, interviewers can get 15 minutes from potential employees about how they used their resources, how they made their decisions, what steps they took, and how well they worked with the customer. This has helped Marriott identify great candidates. The company has also found that group interviewing makes a difference. Having more than one interviewer present affords different views of a candidate. What one interviewer sees, another may not.

BACKGROUND CHECK

Shirley Arline, a human resources consultant, also recommends behavior based interviewing. "Past behavior is the best predictor of future behavior," she says. And what about criminal background checks? "It's worth the $25 to $30 investment. Federal negligent-hiring and retention laws hold you accountable as their employer. If anything happens, the risk of liability is high because the law says you should have known about it."

If you want to have a remarkable business, hire remarkable people. If they're unremarkable, you're invisible, and invisible is boring and unprofitable.

SET HIGH STANDARDS

If you set high standards within your four walls, you will attract employees who thrive under such standards. But even better, high standards repel people with low standards. If they aren't repelled now, they will rebel later. Those who choose mediocre standards have the largest support group. They support each other by buying into each other's excuses and letting each other off the hook.

Employees fail not because they can't do the job, but because they won't. Challenge them. Tell applicants, "We don't have a job for you, but we do have an opportunity for you to make the team."

Know Your Internal Customer

Make sure your internal customers know it's okay to speak out. It doesn't help to have an open-door policy if you don't have an open-ear policy.

Everyone has a complaint department, but nobody has a praise department. Why not open a praise department in your business? Your relationship with your internal customers should be one long conversation. We often forget that business is a game. In sports, players become skillful at handling the ball. As managers, your skill is defined by how you handle conversations. You score points by having conversations that make a difference. To the degree that you become masterful at conversations, you'll become a star player in your business.

Knowing what your internal customers think is essential. We are asked by many clients to conduct internal probes—formalized surveys that help you learn what your internal customers really think and feel. These customized surveys are often eye-openers. They provide the solid information you need to create and target programs to train and motivate your internal customers. By applying the knowledge learned in these studies, we've been able to help clients increase internal satisfaction and performance, pinpoint problems in management and policies, and gain unique insights at a very low cost.

Even if you don't hire an outside consultant to do it, you should conduct internal customer surveys twice a year to find out what your most important people are thinking. Time and time again we see businesses that stay in touch with their internal customers reduce turnover significantly, raise the quality of their product, and improve their hospitality. The internal customer survey is one of the greatest marketing tools you have. I discussed this in detail in Chapter 3.

Training and Motivation

Once you've hired sunshine, you've got to train and motivate. An entire industry is devoted to helping companies develop fancy brochures, videos, programs and the like to convey the culture and practices of the organization.

HOW NORDSTROM DOES IT

Nordstrom, considered one of the world's best retailers, hands every new employee a handbook that is, in fact, a card that reads:

Welcome to Nordstrom. We're glad to have you with the company. Our number one goal is to provide outstanding customer service. Set both your personal and professional goals high. We have great confidence in your ability to achieve them.

Nordstrom Rules. Rule #1—Use your good judgment in all situations. There will be no additional rules. Please feel free to ask your department manager, store manager, or division manager any question at any time.

Effective training is not that complex. It should be simple and focused. It can be as simple as a single sheet of white paper with your mission or vision statement. So many companies would be better off shutting down the training department and burning all the manuals and videos.

Your job is to train people to be themselves.

Too many companies spend too much money on training that doesn't work because there is no accountability. You can commission a high production values video with professional actors and drop $35,000 in a heartbeat. You can roll it out and show it to your employees, but it'll make no difference if there is no accountability.

One of the dirty little secrets of training, orientation, and motivation is that those fancy printed materials often never get read. A client of mine who operates multiple locations reports that his central office mailed out packages of beautiful, motivational training material, only to discover a month or two later that most of the boxes were shoved behind a cabinet, unopened.

The first day on the job is the most important for a new hire, and the first week is the most important week. It's a crime to hire people, pound their heads full of training and motivation, and then shove them out onto the floor assuming you've done your job. People need a lot of validation and gut checks in the beginning.

Even if you've hired trainers to conduct your training program, you or your managers must take the time for individual orientation with your employees. It's a job that should never be delegated to a certified trainer. Get quick and early feedback. Make sure they're engaged with the business and are having a great experience.

Training should be interactive and fun. When people are having fun, it doesn't seem like work. Make them feel important. They are your internal customers, and if they feel like just another product on the shelf, that's what they'll give your customers.

LATERAL TRAINING

Marriott's June Thompson says her company recently looked at its assumptions about career paths and discovered a better way.

In the past, as a new hire at Marriott, you always started out as a front desk clerk, and then moved up to supervisor, and then assistant manager, assistant front office manager, front office manager. You had to go through all those steps before you could move to another division or another department.

We've thrown that out. Now we offer the opportunity to cross-train throughout our brands and within our hotels. We want our associates to be able to choose other career paths within the organization.

That's Neighborhood Marketing, within your four walls, to your internal customers. It's all local, and everything sells.

Marketing to your existing staff is not just about telling them what to do and how to do it. At Hard Rock Café, they've taken the training manual and turned it into a comic book. They are marketing to, and hiring, young people who are visual and want to have fun. They even got some of their employees to help write the content and draw the comics. As a result, the staff of Hard Rock have a direct interest in the training and motivation of new hires.

An unexpected side benefit: the comic-book training manuals have become collector's items, and some Hard Rock employees keep them on their coffee tables at home because they think they look cool.

HERE TODAY, GONE TOMORROW

During the heady days of the 1990s it was difficult for many companies to find and keep staff. It was a seller's market. That's all changed, of course, but turnover remains a big problem in businesses that are seen as entry level career points for many young people. This is a difficult problem to manage, but not impossible if you approach it realistically and with caring.

Supervisors and managers play a crucial role in retaining employees when they take the time to bond with them. If you're in a traditionally high-turnover business, be upfront and honest with your employees: "Look, you're probably going to be with me for about six months. If you are here in six months, you'll get a $50 bonus. But in the meantime, if you give me your all, I'll teach you communications skills and salesmanship skills and give you responsibility, so you'll be a better-qualified candidate for the next job you seek."

That's Neighborhood Marketing to your internal customers. Show that you care, share what you know, and make your staff partners in everything you do.

GROOM OR BROOM

Suppose you find yourself saddled with a one-star employee who isn't getting it and, in the middle of a business rush, is having a bad day, mumbling under his breath, treating customers poorly. What do you do? Try giving him a pat on the back and saying, "Look, I'm not sure what the problem is today, but go in the back and get off the floor for a minute and collect your thoughts. I can't afford to have you irritating my customers like this."

You may be surprised by the dynamic that follows. The employee will typically become defensive—"Oh, I'm all right. My dog ran away"—or give you any of a hundred other excuses for what's wrong.

Stick to your guns and say, "Go to the back, collect your thoughts, and when you're ready to take care of our customers, come back out on the line."

The rest of your staff are going to notice immediately and may even start snickering. But your employee will come back with a different attitude, often enthusiastic and ready to go back to work. That's a way to get a one-star employee up to three stars without spending any money.

Some of your internal customers are never going to rise above one or two stars. That's when you need to invoke marketing expert Jeffrey J. Fox's rule: groom them or broom them. One-star employees are like cancers. If they're not getting it and can't be groomed, you shouldn't be afraid to let them go. The first 30 to 90 days are critical in identifying whether or not you'll be able to develop a new staff member.

Train your supervisors and managers to identify who's performing and who's not, whether an employee is in the right job or not, and use those first 90 days to have talks with your new hires and observe their performance. Once you pass that milestone, it becomes more and more difficult to justify firing them, even if you should.

Take a close look at the turnover rates of your new hires. If turnover rises between 90 and 120 days, you've given your staff false promises. They no longer like you, and they're going on to someone else.

Your managers and supervisors may be asleep at the switch, not paying attention to employee morale and turnover issues. Some of our clients have had success by starting an employee newsletter to communicate training information and motivational messages directly to the frontline. An unanticipated result for one client was that their 18- and 19-year-old employees were asking their supervisors about the training materials they were supposed to have received.

Another tactic in larger organizations is to include body counts in your reports to managers. Show your supervisors how many people are bailing out early, then take the time to explain how costly that is.

WHEN EAGLES ACT LIKE TURKEYS

Many companies know how to hire eagles and even give them pretty good training and support in the art of hospitality. But then they let them say and do the stupidest things. A friend of mine who recently flew from New York to Florida on Delta Airlines reported the following string of shining moments that reflected poorly on the company and its hard-working employees.

At the terminal, in the gate area, flight announcements were made by a person with a thick Spanish accent that rendered the information unintelligible and therefore useless. Aboard the plane, the cabin crew chief announced: "Your pilots today are Jack and Chris, and your attendants include the lovely Julia from Alabama." People who are mostly terrified of flying anyway, and especially so post-9/11, do not want the informality and intimacy suggested by such an announcement. Why are airlines still pretending that flying is fun? It's awful, it's unhealthy, and the best way to market it is to talk about safety, comfort, or some other primal reason to use one airline over another.

Next, the Delta announcer insulted every single passenger by saying, "Now, in case you haven't driven a car since 1952, here's how to operate your seat belt." When he was done with his bored spiel on emergency exits, he quipped, "Can ya tell it's been a long day?"

The flight was delayed getting off the ground, and once the plane was in the air, the pilot came on to tell everyone, "Folks, just so you know, we were lucky to have gotten out only 30 minutes late. Other flights behind us will be an hour and a half late." Chaos! Is that the message Delta wants to convey to its customers?

Finally, in a fit of customer-service euphoria, one of the captains came on to point out that in the sky that night we could see the planet Mars, "which—uhhh—is the closest it's—uhhh—been to earth in—uhhh—a long time—uhhh—thousands and thousands of years."

When people want clownish service, they go to the circus. On an airplane, they want crisp, professional service. They want exactly the information they need, and no more, to get where they're going safely and as close to on time as possible. They don't give a hoot where the lovely Julia is from. They expect to be treated with respect, not insulted. They don't want to know that their lives are in the hands of people who are at the end of a long day and don't have the energy even to convey a spectacular event like the nearness of Mars with more than careless boredom.

A FEW WORDS OF WISDOM

- Make sure your employees understand your business and their role in it.

- Share information with them: how much things cost, your revenue, your goals, your mission. Let them know when business is good, and ask their advice when it isn't.

- Never stop recruiting. The moment you do is when key people quit.

- Help your internal customers think in terms of their future, not yours.

- Invest in training. A good place to start is 1 percent of gross revenues.

- Instead of trying to come up with something new and clever, do what you do best.

- Communicate your values and expectations through your actions. Lead by example.

- Show me the love! Employees are living advertisments. Your company's message is its people. Every person in your company is a message. Every marketing plan begins with your internal customers. The choice is yours, the time is now. Think small—act fast—stay fresh. Stretch to grow—ask questions—think results.

CHAPTER 7

PLAN TO IMPLEMENT YOUR PLAN

*The most pathetic person in the world is
someone who has sight but no vision.*

HELEN KELLER

CHAPTER 7

A FRIEND OF MINE TELLS THE STORY of visiting an Olive Garden restaurant in the Midwest during an evening rush. There was a wait, and while he lingered in the lobby he noticed that the restaurant had an attractive refrigerated display case containing samples of items from the menu, including an antipasto salad. He loved antipasto! He went over to have a closer look only to discover that the entire plate of food was covered with mold.

Not only was he repelled in the moment, the experience soured his opinion of Olive Garden as a place where he might want to eat in the future, and he's been telling that story for 10 years.

It's amazing how often managers and employees don't see what's right in front of them, even when it's costing them.

YOUR WHITE-GLOVE INSPECTION

So you've come up with some good promotional ideas and put a lot of work into being creative, budgeting money for great materials, and now you're going to hand your Neighborhood Marketing plan to your frontline, where it will succeed or fail depending on how well they execute.

Hold on a second. Before you launch your promotion, make sure you're prepared to meet your customers' expectations. You wouldn't invite people to your house for a party and not clean it before you get started. You'd get some fresh flowers, make sure you had enough plates and utensils, and do everything you could, right up until the doorbell rings, to make sure the party is a success. And remember, everything they see may end up social media before they even finish their meal!

Great marketing can kill your business if you aren't prepared.

In this next section I'll talk about details, mainly in the context of food service, but many of these principles apply in any kind of business. Even if you're in a service or consulting business, there are a host of things to think about. Who answers the phone, and how friendly does she sound? How clear is your message? Do your employees have answers to every question? If not, do they understand that they should never say, "I don't know," but instead, "Let me find someone who can answer that"?

You need to ask yourself: What will my customers' experience be? What will they see, smell, taste, hear, and feel? Killing your efforts with a bad first impression is much easier than you can imagine.

Start outside your four walls, at your property line. If you haven't done it recently, get the parking lot lines restriped. Fix the potholes. Have the landscaping updated. Make sure every scrap of litter is picked up. Cut out the dead parts of your hedges.

Ray Kroc was a big proponent of lush landscaping. At a recent marketing conference we ran, Ed Rensi told our audience about his experiences with the company's philosophy:

In the early days we had red-and-white-tiled buildings and we took glass wax and waxed our buildings once a week. I can't tell you how many Tuesday nights I waxed that building.

I was a store manager in Jamestown, New York, and in the summer we had bugs galore up there. So we decided to put yellow fluorescent fixtures and yellow bulbs in all the incandescent fixtures. We had yellow bulbs everywhere, hoping the bugs would not be attracted. But the bugs turned out to like all kinds of light. I used fly swatters and bug spray. But the restaurant looked dirty when I did that.

So I got rid of all the yellow light bulbs and I got some bright white bulbs. The bugs still came, but I cleaned them up every day. It was more work, but the restaurant looked better.

I discovered that clean bathrooms make food taste better. If you don't have a clean bathroom and you don't keep it clean and keep it odor-free, your customer thinks, How can the kitchen be clean? Because if you don't have time to clean the bathrooms, you probably don't have time to clean the kitchen.

I engaged in toilet marketing. I once gave a speech to 8,000 McDonald's franchisees, and the sole subject was clean bathrooms. If your customers walk into your restaurant and they can smell it before they see it, you have a problem. You should put ice in the urinals to keep the waste from fermenting and the smell from proliferating. You should put perfume spritzers that activate themselves every couple of minutes.

If I wanted to build a restaurant today, I would put nothing but white tile and white walls in the bathroom. I would put four 4-bulb fluorescent fixtures in that bathroom. I would make it as bright and white and light as I possibly could to prove that it is sanitary. And when I got done scrubbing it, I would use some chlorine-based solution to sanitize it and make it smell clean. I guarantee your customers are going to think your food tastes better.

In the restaurants I managed, we had 2,000 people a day using our restrooms. We used 14 rolls of toilet paper a day. If you can measure it, you can manage it. We understood by keeping track of such things that our customers were spending a lot of time in there. This is so simplistic it's almost embarrassing to explain it.

In managing these restaurants, Ed said he learned exactly how many flowers it takes to create a satisfying display. "Too many is exactly the right amount. People love the lushness of spring. Your customers want to see four seasons. Lots of flowers is an inexpensive marketing tool. The simple things work best."

Everything sells.

POLICE THE GROUNDS

Work your way through all the zones of your business. Try to imagine what it's like to see it for the first time. (If you have trouble doing this, ask someone else to do it for you.) Are there cigarette butts ground out in front of the door? Gum stuck on the sidewalk? Trash in the gutter? Is the glass smudged with fingerprints? Is the awning torn, faded, dusty? Are your signs clean and freshly painted, or did letters disappear in the last wind storm? Put a fresh coat of paint on your building, or at least touch up the trim.

Everything sells.

Do your displays look fresh and bountiful, or is the stuff tired and crusty? If you're offering a dessert tray, make sure the samples are fresh. If they're getting dry and you haven't quite made it to the end of the day, throw them out anyway and either make up a fresh tray or don't show it.

In any business using printed materials, make sure they aren't dog eared, smudged, or faded. Restaurants go through thousands of menus, and I often find they haven't noticed when the photographs have become faded from use and sunlight or there are food stains. Paper products are cheap and should be changed as often as necessary to maintain a crisp, clean impression.

Is your tire store's waiting room smeared with grease and dirt? Is the coffee table piled with outdated, coffee-stained magazines?

Do people entering your clothing store have to dodge carts full of merchandise being reshelved? Are shoppers in your grocery in constant danger of being run over by stock carts?

When customers enter your restaurant, do they hear rattling dishes or hollering from the back? Are they greeted at the front door by a warm, engaged, hospitality-oriented person? Is the welcome heartfelt, or is it mechanical and cold?

Do waiting customers have to stand in a cold, cramped foyer next to a cash register, or can they sit on a plush sofa next to a vase of flowers and enjoy soft music and the aroma of fine cuisine wafting in the air? The atmosphere should be pleasant but not bland.

Does your hostess interact with children, ask questions, make your customers feel important? Does she walk guests to their table at a comfortable pace, or does she leave them in the dust?

How many times have you walked into a restaurant and the host or hostess barks at you: "Hi! Two? Smoking or non?" Or, if you're alone: "One? Oh!"—as if you're a disappointment or a loser? Your customers get a huge part of their impression of you in the first few seconds of their experience. You don't want to have to spend the rest of the time making up for a bad beginning.

Everything sells.

The best time to engage customers is when they first walk through your door. Have your receptionist, sales staff, host or hostess come out from behind the podium, desk, or counter and interact with the customer. The greeter should open the door and take one or two steps toward the customer, offer a handshake, notice a beautiful blouse or a colorful tie, and determine whether the customer is a regular or a first time visitor. The best greeters in the business are those whose memory allows them to address regulars by name and remember new names from the start.

What does your business, any business, smell like when customers first arrive? If you keep your business extra clean, does it smell like disinfectant? If you have an odor problem, don't cover it up with perfume—buy an air purifier. This device creates a fresh, clean, just-after-the-thunderstorm smell and defeats just about any unpleasant odor you can imagine.

In a restaurant, is the food hot or lukewarm? Is cold wine served cold? Every detail counts, and customers remember the details – and share them.

MARSHAL YOUR SALES FORCE

Look around your business. Who can you recruit for a marketing committee? Which employees should represent what areas of your business? If you've got a month-long promotion that starts next month, each department needs to know what it is supposed to do. This helps employees take ownership in the process—and when they do, they'll sell it to their peers better than management ever could.

Before you run your promotion, write up a detailed description of how it's going to work and hand it out to all of your employees so they know exactly what's expected of them. This also makes them better marketing partners and able to answer questions from customers about what's going on.

Build incentives for employees into each marketing program so they receive some direct benefit from making it a success. If you don't have enough people to run the promotion, increase staffing levels.

Build a sense of urgency into your promotion by setting an expiration date. But don't let your staff get so rigid that they refuse to serve people the day after it ends. The customer knows the expiration date has expired—he's just waiting to see how you're going to handle it. Be gracious. See it as an opportunity to win over another customer.

BE CLEAR IN YOUR TACTICS

As I've said before, I'm not a big fan of percentage discounts, except in certain, well-designed promotions like the in-store fortune cookie program. Customers have trouble understanding percentage discounts; dollars off is a more effective incentive. And don't fall into the trap of discounting over and over again. If you get your customers addicted to discounts, you'll find they won't come to you unless you offer a discount.

In your promotions, don't give with the big print and take away with the small. Don't impose complex or impossible conditions. Don't get halfway through the promotion, realize it's harder than you thought, and change the rules midstream.

If you haven't thought through all these issues ahead of time, your staff could develop a negative attitude. Make sure you don't set them—and your plans—up for failure.

TIME YOUR MOVES

There is an old expression in marketing that many businesspeople ignore at their peril: Fish when the fish are biting. This is one of the hardest things for us to understand as marketers, because our instinct is to try to fix what we think is wrong. If you try to increase sales on Monday and Tuesday when business is going to be slow anyway, you squander the opportunity to fish when the fish are biting. If weekends are your busy time, that's obviously when people have an urge to spend. Run your promotion then to leverage the opportunity you already have.

I sometimes suggest running a promotion on Mother's Day. Clients look at me as if I had lost my mind. Yes, it's the busiest day of the year, but unless you're truly swamped, why wouldn't you seize the opportunity to introduce new customers to your business? A busy day like that is a terrific opportunity to promote something else. Give a bounce-back guest certificate.

All the same, be sure your promotions are time-appropriate. Motorists aren't interested in an air conditioning tune-up in the dead of winter.

Don't forget to build in lead times for every aspect of your promotion. On your calendar, mark deadlines for each part of the planning process. If you're running one unit of a chain, don't forget to check for conflicting corporate or regional promotions. There is nothing more frustrating: you're totally absorbed in your marketing plans, things are going smoothly, you've got a great promotion teed up—only to discover, a week before your kickoff date, that your corporate office is about to launch a monster promotion of its own that's going to swamp your boat.

Even without the head office jumping in, do you have too much going on at one time? How often have you gone into a store to buy something and been bombarded with 10 promotions going on at once? On the board outside there's one message, and inside is a banner that says something else, and then you get to the table or the counter and there's yet another promotion. Don't confuse your customer; keep your promotion focused and organized. Be especially wary of big holidays. They can make or break you.

What about scheduling two or more promotions at the same time? Check the practice in your industry, but we have found that, in general, this can be a recipe for disaster. It's best to focus your efforts and avoid competing with yourself.

Give your staff a break between promotions. It's hard to keep getting pumped for promotions one after another if you don't have a rest. Your customers need a rest, too. It's counterproductive to give them the impression that a special event is business as usual, because normal operations then become something for them to avoid. They'll just wait a few days until the next big special comes along.

ZONE MERCHANDISING

Whenever you start thinking about a promotion, divide your business into merchandising zones. (I'll go into more detail in Chapter 13, but here's a quick run-through.) Start by making a diagram of your store, a blueprint. Identify the zones, from the curb to the bathrooms. Think of each zone as a message center. What's the message? Figure out how you're going to use each zone to make it a success.

Think of your business as a nonstop infomercial. If you were going to make a training video for your stores and use your store as the place to shoot it, think about what you would need to do to make it look good. A week before your promotion starts, you should be painting, replacing, fixing, and cleaning, and you should be reminding your staff to come to work with clean clothes and fresh haircuts.

Zone merchandising turns your business into a media weapon over which you have total control. Inside your store, your customers are a captive audience. There's no remote; they can't switch channels or mute the sound. It's more effective than internet, radio, television, or print because you own their senses. You're the host for their experience, and it's up to you to put the message into play. What will the message be each day, and how well are you influencing that message?

CHAPTER 8

WIN THE CUSTOMERS
IN YOUR BACKYARD

Opportunity is a bird that never perches.

CLAUDE MCDONALD, MANAGEMENT EXPERT

CHAPTER 8

IN MY WORK I TRAVEL CONSTANTLY. I spend hundreds of nights in hotel rooms and eat thousands of meals in hotel restaurants. I'm worth about $500,000 in food, beverage, and room charges annually.

But no hotel has ever called me and asked me for my business.

I live a quarter mile from a chain grocery store. I'd estimate that I'm probably worth about $10,000 a year or so in grocery store food purchases.

But no one has ever asked me to come in and do my shopping at that store, which is not just in my neighborhood but practically in my backyard.

For the savvy, thinking neighborhood marketer, the customers to grow your business are right next door, just waiting to be asked to do business with you. All it takes is a little thought and effort.

A young man I know of had worked for several years for a unit of a national chain of sign shops. He finally learned enough to feel competent at his trade, and grew tired enough of working for someone else to go into business for himself.

He knew from studying the store he worked in that the customers who needed signs most frequently were new businesses and, in this fast-growing suburb of Philadelphia, the construction industry. He also knew there were five other sign shops in the area he'd have to compete with, not including his previous employer.

He contacted the state corporations department and got a list of all the new incorporations that had been filed in the past year. He sorted the list to pull out those in his trading area and sent them all a mailing, offering his services.

He also contacted the local building trades association and sent a different mailing to all of its members, offering quick turnaround for the signage they use to mark and announce new projects. In a couple of months he had more business than he could handle.

A recent client of mine is a large retail chain with 1,850 stores nationwide. One year the company spent $15 million on mass media, but the results did not meet their goals. The next year, they fired the national creative agency and all the regional ad agencies and committed their marketing budget to an innovative campaign.

On March 30, our kickoff date, 10,000 promotional direct-mail pieces were sent to every home within a three-mile radius of each unit in the country.

The next month, two Neighborhood Marketing ambassadors per unit personally visited every business within a one-mile radius of each of the 1,850 stores. To add more fun and excitement to the campaign, if the ambassadors could smell fresh bread or freshly baked cookies when they entered the local businesses, they gave a $20 gift card to the employees in the store.

Simultaneously, we had hospitality coaches visit each unit to teach the principles of friendliness and how to smile and greet customers with genuine warmth. We provided the hospitality coaches with a custom-painted Hospitality Van. When the employees at each unit saw the van pull into their lot, they knew it was their turn to participate in the campaign and were empowered by the training. The campaign was a complete success, with unit sales up across the board.

THINK LOCAL

The battle for the hearts and minds of consumers is won block by block, store by store, and purchase by purchase. Rather than putting up a billboard, visit a different business in your neighborhood each day and bring it a gift from your shop.

If you don't have time yourself, appoint a Captain Hook on your staff, someone with outstanding people skills, a complete knowledge of your business and its products and services, and have him or her spend an hour or so each day visiting neighborhood businesses.

If you own a restaurant, deliver free lunches or desserts to the employees of the business you're visiting that day. If you run a retail shop, deliver a sampling of what you sell or are currently promoting. If you operate a window-washing service, wash their front windows for free. If you own a spa, offer a five-minute shoulder massage. The possibilities are limited only by your creativity and initiative.

Start a new homeowners program to win the business of people who are new to your community. Smartleads, Inc., is a company based in Tampa, Florida, (see Appendix B for contact information) that provides targeted address lists and mailing services to as many as millions of recipients or as few as 50. They offer affordable, customized, four-color direct mail pieces to send to new homeowners in your trading area.

One way to both reach new customers and bring in your regulars is to run an ad in your neighborhood paper offering $5 to anyone who can find an intentional spelling error you've included in the text. Most readers look only at headlines, so write one that compels them to read the whole ad: "There's a spelling error in this ad. If you spot it, we'll give you $5."

Put the error deep in the ad so readers will get your marketing message before discovering how to claim the reward. Make the reward an appropriate amount toward a purchase, based on the average prices of your products or services. Don't make it look like a discount or coupon. Instead, make it look like a gift certificate. If your product or service sells for hundreds, you may want to make the certificate worth $50 or $100.

Create a preferred-patron bounce-back promotion to increase awareness, frequency, and traffic. Produce "funny money" bills or certificates that customers can use on their next visit to your business. Make the denominations worth about 10 percent of your average transaction. If customers spend an average of $40, give them $4 in bounce-back bills or certificates.

This promotion works well because it's unadvertised, a surprise that creates word-of-mouth exposure especially once the experience is shared on social media. To ensure the return business, give your funny money an expiration date of 30 days.

THINK SMALL

Like an old bucket, traditional marketing springs leaks you can plug only by understanding your customers and using effective retention techniques to cut down on defections. Don't swing for the grand slam every time. Businesses are built in increments, so aim for small gains and increases, and build on them again and again.

The promise of success in retail, service, and hospitality industries is greater than ever, because customers are fed up with bad service and bad marketing. All you have to do is let them know you're prepared to treat them as important, valued human beings.

When Wal-Mart or another big-box category-killer store moves to a new town, the local businesspeople freak out. Hardware stores, bookstores, independent grocers, and pharmacists feel helpless and vulnerable against the powerful marketing resources of these giants.

But every crisis is an opportunity, and American consumers are catching on to some of the dirty little secrets of mega-retailing. One is that, overall, prices at big-box stores are not that much lower than at the neighborhood merchant. Another is that big-box stores can never offer the personal touch that Neighborhood Marketing offers in the hands of the local retailer. Your local Home Depot store manager is probably not a member of your Chamber of Commerce, and the manager of the nearest Barnes & Noble is not likely anytime soon to walk into your business and offer you a free book.

This is the secret of fighting the big-box stores. You fight them by using all the techniques you've learned so far, by building lasting relationships with the people who live in your trading area, and by building loyalty among the customers already inside your four walls.

MYSTERIOUS DISCOUNTS

One tactic I recommend to local entrepreneurs is called Mystery Night. Choose a traditionally slower night of the week and establish a specific time frame, such as 6 to 8 P.M., to run your promotion. For those two hours, you discount everything you sell 50 percent or more.

This works best for lower-ticket businesses like small cafés, movie rentals, car washes, and ice-cream shops, but it can be adapted to work well in restaurants and shops with higher-ticket items as well. The higher ticket your item, the shorter your sale time should be.

One store selling fine jewelry runs this promotion as Mystery Hour. Each month, it sets an hour, such as 10 to 11 A.M. on a particular Tuesday, during which customers shopping in the store get 50 percent off any item. The key to this promotion's success is that it is run at random times without notice. Nobody knows when it's going to happen—but when it does, everyone talks about it!

Let customers know you plan to have a Mystery Night or a Mystery Hour at least once a month on one of your slowest nights, and that it will always be a surprise. By following this formula, you can turn some of your slowest nights into some of your strongest.

"GOTCHA" TICKETS

Here's another customer-pleasing event that's effective: Canvas your trading area with a Parking Ticket Summons promotion that generates awareness, increases positive public relations, and drives up sales. A lawn and garden shop in San Antonio, Texas, printed a promotional card that, from a distance, looked like a standard yellow parking ticket. It sent a staff member out with a sack of quarters to feed any meter that had expired and to slip a card under the car's windshield wipers.

Here's what the card said:

RELAX! This is NOT a parking ticket. We just happened to be going by your car and noticed that the meter had expired. To save you the hassle and cost of a fine, we've taken the liberty of putting a little bit of money in the meter for you. Compliments of The Lawn and Garden Shop.

This promotion triggered a lot of attention and an avalanche of word of mouth advertising! The lawn and garden shop received a flurry of phone calls, including some from the media—and one from the San Antonio Police Department. As it turned out, because of a policy not to ticket the same car twice, true violations were going unnoticed. To continue its promotion and keep the peace, the lawn and garden shop changed the color of its promotional card to blue.

PEOPLE

The best things in life are not "things" but memories of great experiences. In fact, when people were asked to rank their preferences, they ranked experiences with other people far above goods and services. This ranking reflects the human need for a sense of place and a feeling of significance. As Barbra Streisand so memorably sang, "People who need people are the luckiest people in the world." If your employees fail to remember this, there's another Streisand song that may express your regrets: "The Way We Were."

HIDDEN PRIZES

Another winning tactic is the Scratch-Off Mailer. This one works well with multiple stores. It's a flyer containing mystery gift certificates, with the offer hidden under scratchable ink. You mail the flyers to your database, with instructions that the offer is good only if the customer comes into the store, where your employee will scratch it to reveal the value of the offer.

If you don't have multiple locations, you can make this program a success by partnering with noncompeting businesses that share your trade area or target customer base, such as stores in a nearby shopping center.

If you're in auto sales, have your ad agency create a newspaper ad with a message, hidden in the printed design that can be deciphered only by holding a special plastic sheet over it. To discover the hidden message and claim their prize—a $500 shopping spree at a grocery store, say, or a weekend hotel getaway—readers would have to bring the puzzle to your dealership.

And here's the kicker: you put the plastic decoder sheet on the rearview mirror inside the cars you want to sell. The customer has to sit inside a car in order to decode the message. It's simple, it drives an enormous amount of traffic with the promise of a big prize, and, best of all, it gets your potential customers inside the car.

Uncommon managers are creative, caring, and passionate individuals who understand that they are rewarded for what their people do. What would it feel like to channel energy, passion, and enthusiasm into every human being who works for you or buys from you? Would you be able to come to work every morning committed to making a positive difference in people's lives, so filled with light and enthusiasm that you would brighten up the work space? Great managers come to work focused and inspired, ready to create the best day possible and to lead their team toward excellence.

You don't have to officially manage other people in your workplace; by simply interacting with others, you affect their energies, their motivation, and their passion. Of course, there will be days when this is not so, when you're down, but great managers make those the exceptions.

XTREME SERVICE

Small-business owners enjoy several advantages over the big companies, because the big guys are grasping at straws and throwing more money at media instead of speaking to the neighborhood. Be willing to do whatever it takes to keep your current customers delighted and coming back for more, even if it means refunding their money when you think you shouldn't. Guarantees mean everything to customers. You've got to make your offers risk-free.

Are you in the habit of arguing with unhappy customers? Sure, you may avoid shelling out good money to confused or mistaken or unscrupulous people, but what about all the good, honest customers who should have come back for refunds and adjustments but didn't, because they'd rather not have a confrontation? Surprise people with unexpectedly great service. They'll tell their friends and family, and you'll gain more than you lose.

As a small-business operator, you can steal a page from big companies like Nordstrom, Sears, and L.L. Bean, which are famous for their return policies. A friend bought a pair of shoes at Nordstrom's several years ago, got them home, put them on, and discovered they were just a little too tight. He felt like an idiot for not taking time to test-walk the shoes in the store, so he put them in a closet and forgot about them.

A year went by, and he decided to purchase a new pair of shoes. He went back to Nordstrom's because he liked their selection of styles and the service. He announced to the clerk that he wanted to try several sizes, because he'd bought a pair that ended up being too tight.

"Bring them back," the clerk said.

"But I bought them a year ago."

"Doesn't matter," the clerk replied. "Bring them back and I'll give you full credit."

The word-of-mouth advertising that comes from transactions like that is worth more than all the slick advertising Nordstrom's could have bought.

THINK SMALL, LIKE WAL-MART

You may be in competition with Wal-Mart, but that doesn't mean you can't steal some of their good ideas. Sam Walton, founder and CEO, said his first rule of retailing was "Think one store at a time." In his autobiography he illustrated what he meant:

We've got one store in Panama City, Florida, and another only five miles away in Panama City Beach; but actually they are worlds apart when it comes to their merchandise mix and their customer base. They're entirely different kinds of stores. One is built for tourists going to the beach, and the other is more like the normal Wal-Mart, built for folks who live in town.

Focusing on a single store can accomplish a number of things. First, of course, it enables us to actually improve that store. But if, in the process, we also happen to learn a particular way in which the Panama City Beach Wal-Mart is outsmarting the competition on, say, beach towels, then we can quickly get the information out to all our beach stores around the country and see if the approach works everywhere.

Thinking small works because every market is unique. Every customer wants something different. To give each customer what he or she wants, you must act locally.

One of our clients operated two stores in New York City, about 100 yards apart, selling the same brands. One store had been open for 76 years, the other for 40. The two marketing plans we wrote were 80 percent different: the older store catered to the tourist market, the newer store to locals.

To market and promote the store that catered to tourists, we worked with hotel concierges, with cabbies, and in every other tourist venue we could think of to reach people who were visiting New York.

To market the newer store across the street, we made personal visits to deliver products and samples to other retail stores within a two- or three-block radius, targeting the 200,000 people who worked and lived there. We ran direct-mail and bounce-back programs constantly. Both stores flourished by catering to different markets in the same trading neighborhood. Each store's marketing strategy was in alignment with its customer base.

REWARD LOCALLY

Customers have different needs. You must have an effective way of responding to those needs. This requires a committed, responsive staff at the local level, because the top company people, off somewhere else at corporate headquarters, don't know the local product mix, service, store hours, delivery, or staff requirements the way you do in your own neighborhood.

The execution of strategy relies mainly on the people you hire and train, who are always local. The scarcest, most critical resource for winning the local market is a skilled, committed, focused staff and frontline managers. Strive to create a work environment where staff input, autonomy, and accountability create rather than dissipate energy. Recognize your employees' birthdays by sending them cards and gift certificates. Give them something special on their wedding anniversaries. Enclose inspirational messages or notes with their paychecks telling them you appreciate them. For performing high-quality work, meeting schedules, even for showing up consistently and on time, award staff members a "Get Out of Work Free" card that's redeemable with seven days' advance notice.

Your employees are your internal customers, your first customers. Without their support, loyalty, and enthusiasm, you won't have the success you seek with your second customers, your guests, and patrons.

CHAPTER 9

MARKET TO YOUR EMPLOYEES

My whole philosophy is that we build men.
Incidentally, we move freight.

ARTHUR IMPERATORE,
PRESIDENT, A-P-A TRANSPORT

Chapter 9

YOU MAY THINK YOU KNOW HOW to motivate your employees, but what you probably haven't fully realized yet is that they are your first and often most important customers. Here's a true story that so powerfully illustrates this notion that it's repeated from stages and pulpits across the land.

Captain J. Charles Plumb, a 1964 graduate of the U.S. Naval Academy, had flown 74 combat missions over Vietnam when his luck ran out on the 75th, just five days before he was to return home. His plane was felled by a missile. He was captured and spent the next 2,103 days as a prisoner of war in brutal Communist prison camps.

He survived, and many years later, sitting in a restaurant in Kansas City, he noticed that an unfamiliar man two tables away was staring at him. After a few minutes, the man stood and approached Plumb's table, pointing his finger in Plumb's face and declaring, "You're Captain Plumb!"

The ex-pilot was shocked.

The stranger went on, "You flew jet fighters in Vietnam. You were on the aircraft carrier Kitty Hawk. You were shot down. You parachuted into enemy hands and spent six years as a prisoner of war."

"How in the world did you know all that?" Plumb asked.

"Because I packed your parachute."

Plumb leaped to his feet to shake the man's hand. "I guess it worked," the sailor said.

"I must tell you I've said a lot of prayers of thanks for your nimble fingers," Plumb recalls, "but I never thought I'd have the opportunity to express my gratitude in person."

Plumb had trouble sleeping that night. He kept thinking about that man. He wondered what the man might have looked like in a Navy uniform— a Dixie cup hat, a bib in the back, bell-bottom trousers. He wondered how many times he might have passed this man aboard the Kitty Hawk—how many times he might have seen him and not even said "Good morning," "How are you?" or anything, because Plumb was a fighter pilot, and this man was just a sailor. Plumb recalls wondering, "How many hours did he spend on that long wooden table in the bowels of that ship, weaving the shrouds and folding the silks of those chutes? I couldn't have cared less—until one day my parachute came along and he packed it for me."

Who's packing your parachute? And whose parachute should you be packing?

FIRST-CUSTOMER MARKETING

Marketing to your staff is every bit as important as marketing to your customers. Your staff are your marketing ambassadors. Give every employee who works for you, right down to the dishwasher, his or her own business card and the incentive to use it. Suddenly you've got a salesperson in every barber shop, gas station, and family event in your neighborhood.

Every employee should be provided with gift certificates and discount coupons to share with family, friends, and neighbors. Every employee should be part of incentive programs and contests that are designed to sell products and increase sales.

Remember: it's costly and time-consuming to find eagles and keep them. Identify your eagles and help them soar. It's good for business and good for life. It's Neighborhood Marketing, using your four walls.

THE PERSONAL CONNECTION

One essential for increasing sales is to get people to spend more when they come in. Here's a foolproof way to help your staff promote an item: have them wear buttons that say, "If I don't suggest X, it's free!" X can be an ice cream cone, a power drill, a bouquet of flowers, an oil change, or whatever product you're promoting.

Sometimes it's just a matter of getting your employees to show an interest in, and some empathy for, your customers. On my way to give a speech recently, I had dinner, registered at my hotel, and began to unpack my clothes for the next morning. To my horror, I realized I had packed a formal shirt that required cuff links. I did not have any cuff links.

I ran to my car, drove to the nearest Wal-Mart, went to the jewelry counter, and discovered the store did not sell cuff links. I raced to a Target, dashed in past an attendant who was starting to lock the doors, got to the jewelry counter, and asked for cuff links. The clerk said she had never heard the term.

I leaned against the counter, tired, frustrated, and disappointed. The lady asked me what she could do to help me. That's all it took. I told her the whole story about how I was going to be speaking at this important event. She looked at me and asked, "Why don't you just buy another shirt?" I woke up from my daze and said, "That's a hell of an option!"

THE FEEL-GOOD FACTOR

A profitable way to promote your business and empower your staff is to create a custom newspaper for your business that promotes your strengths and your team of employees. This is easy to do in four-page advertorial format that looks like USA Today, and it's an effective piece to hand or mail to your customers and display in your store. You can even do an electronic version that can be shared.

If you aren't already running internal contests for your staff, start now. Launch an employee challenge program. Give each employee 50 to 100 flyers of your menu of products or services, with the employee's name on the back. Ask them to distribute the flyers outside your store—at businesses, homes, gatherings. When customers come in, tally up the names on their flyers and award a big prize to the winning employee. Make sure the prize is something that everyone will want!

Why go to so much trouble to involve your employees and keep them happy? Because if your employees are not happy with their work environment, how can you expect the customers who come through your doors to be satisfied? Your employees pass their attitude right along to the customer. It's up to you to hire good people and treat them well, so they will pass on enthusiasm and excitement, rather than boredom and discontent.

THE CAN-DO PRINCIPLE

More than anything else, customers hate being told, "We can't do that," or "I'm not authorized," or "I don't know," or "It's against our policy." Oceans of business have been lost in the instant it takes for a comment like that to make a customer feel powerless and uncared for. If you really want your employees to take pride and ownership in your business, you must give them the authority to do anything to please the customer. This type of marketing focus is one of the most underexploited areas in most businesses.

When I tell other business owners this, they flinch. Most of us give our frontline employees tremendous responsibility, but no authority. We don't trust them. We don't empower them to make decisions. To do something out of the ordinary for a customer, they have to find a boss and get approval. It's demeaning for the employee, frustrating for the customer, and just plain bad for business.

Ritz-Carlton Hotels has given all its frontline employees spending authority up to $2,000 to take care of a customer's needs. A member of the housecleaning staff can offer a dissatisfied guest a complete refund on his room. When a guest in one of the hotel restaurants isn't pleased with her meal, the server can refund the guest's money on the spot and give her a certificate for a free dinner.

When employees are empowered to make customer-service decisions on the spot, their self-esteem goes up, and so does their pride and ownership in the company. The person who made the complaint feels better and is more likely to become a repeat customer. One of the highest values customers look for is a satisfaction guarantee.

Too often we cage up an employee behind the front desk, make the counter too high, the information confusing or wrong, the room too hot or too cold, then wonder why she can't function. Why not understand what the customers want, set the standard, and involve the employees in creating the process? With this approach, everyone becomes warm and friendly and everyone knows how to up-sell. Stop trying to manage individual employees. You lead people; you manage processes.

Remember my friend George, with the linen store? One thing we did was work with his employees to get them motivated. Many of his staff had been there for years, doing the same old thing the same old way. Much of George's initial success in business came from happy customers. He is a delightful, warm person. But somehow, George's interest in and care for his customers had not rubbed off on his staff. He wasn't packing their parachutes for them.

"George," I said, "we need to create some happiness." And that's what we did. We threw a painting party with the employees to give the walls a fresh coat of paint. We encouraged his employees to come to work in different outfits each day rather than a uniform. I talked him into starting a sales incentive program.

Within months, pride began to grow in George's store. I'd walk in the door and be greeted with a warm smile instead of a sigh or a grimace. Everything started to shift. The dynamics were positive. Business picked up.

Gifted bosses don't manage people. They manage expectations, atmosphere, and emotions. How do you manage expectations and atmosphere? You hire people who like to work, and give them work they like to do.

10 GOOD WAYS TO KEEP EMPLOYEES HAPPY

1. Ask them for their input.

2. Give them incentive to grow.

3. Keep them informed about decisions that affect them.

4. Be flexible in accommodating their personal needs.

5. Empower them to give superior service.

6. Welcome their new ideas.

7. Listen to their complaints.

8. Reward them for good behavior.

9. Hire happy people.

10. Pay them well!

CHAPTER 10

MARKET TO YOUR EXISTING CUSTOMERS

There is only one boss. The customer. And he can fire everybody in the company from the chairman on down, simply by spending his money somewhere else.

SAM WALTON, FOUNDER, WAL-MART

Chapter 10

ALTHOUGH NO HOTEL HAS EVER CALLED and asked me for my business, I once had an extraordinary experience at a hotel that made me a loyal customer. I was staying at a Marriott in Atlanta, where I was scheduled to give a speech the next day. I'd left a wake-up call for seven o'clock.

At exactly seven the phone rang and a woman on the other end, not a machine, announced, "Good morning, Mr. Feltenstein. It's seven o'clock. It's 70 degrees outside, a beautiful day here in Atlanta. I see that you're checking out today. Where are you going next?"

I told her I was scheduled to fly to Fargo, North Dakota.

I heard fingers stroking keys in the background as she said, "Let me look up what the weather is in Fargo. It's about 40 degrees and raining. Can't you stay another day with us in Atlanta? There's so much to do here, and the weather's so lovely."

I was so intrigued, I asked her name. She said it was Sally.

"Well, Sally, the next time I come to Atlanta, I know where I'm going to be staying. Thank you very much!"

Neighborhood Marketing and four-walls promotion is all about mining the gold that's already in your business. I was gold. Sally was an eagle, not a turkey. And Marriott had clearly trained her in the art of building customer loyalty. No advertising dollars were spent, no fancy direct-mail pieces were printed, no postage costs incurred. Just a 60-second phone call, and I tell this story over and over again in my speeches all over the country. I didn't spend the money for a second night, but I became a marketing machine for this Marriott Hotel.

BUILDING CUSTOMER LOYALTY

Once you have put the systems and practices into place to create a fun, exciting work atmosphere and plenty of incentives for your employees, the next focus is your current customer.

The customers you already have are as vital to the success of your operation as the dollars you mustered to open your business. To understand this new perspective, think in terms of the value a single current customer brings to your business. Consider this example: one customer, visiting your operation twice a week and spending as little as $8 per visit, is worth $832 per year in revenue. More important, that customer will probably bring in at least one new customer. Thus, a single repeat customer plus his referral are worth $1,664 a year or, over a decade, $16,640.

A current customer who purchases $200 worth of product or services each month brings about $24,000 to your business over 10 years. One new customer leads to another, and another, and the profits begin to pile up. The same principle applies to your internal customer. What is the value of a long-term employee versus a short-term one?

BEYOND SATISFACTION

A powerful key to the success of your business is your ability to build and retain a large base of loyal customers. Besides providing the obvious rewards of increased profits generated by repeat business, loyal customers are the apostles who spread the good word about you to their friends and acquaintances. Consider the potential of having 70 percent of your customer base working as an unpaid sales force. Think of the numbers of new customers this word-of-mouth advertising could generate.

Fifty percent of advertising is word-of-mouth. What's the word on you?

Great products and superior service aren't enough. A recent survey conducted by the firm Bain & Company determined that a satisfied customer isn't necessarily a loyal one. In fact, the survey revealed that three out of four customers who said they were satisfied with a company's products or services still went elsewhere to buy the same products.

The essential ingredient, after great products and service, is a successful loyalty program that gives your patrons a reason to return and sparks an enduring romance between you and your customers. A poorly run loyalty program may spark initial customer passion, but the attraction will be short-lived, a summer fling instead of the real thing.

NUTS AND BOLTS OF LOYALTY PROGRAMS

Here's what's needed for a successful loyalty program:

1. It must meet the changing needs of your customers. Loyalty programs have a limited shelf life. They are effective only until competitors catch up to you or consumer expectations change. You must evaluate and update your program regularly to make it bigger, better, and faster-acting.

2. It must be easy for customers to participate in and easy for you to track.

3. It must offer rewards that have real value to your customers.

Beyond these basic qualities, your loyalty program should take into account the following five principles:

1. The value you deliver must exceed the cost of delivering it.

2. Customers are not created equal. You must provide the best value to the best customers.

3. Customers should be given a clear understanding of the benefits attached.

4. Your program must not rely on short-term promotions. These can only be part of a larger program.

5. The program must be in line with the brand and relevant to the customer. It should capitalize on an existing emotional connection to the brand and provide benefits that support the signature qualities of the brand.

Consider entering into a loyalty program partnership with other businesses. Partnerships provide a competitive advantage, are attractive to customers, capitalize on buying behavior, and offer the added value of variety in the reward structure. Partnerships capture customers' imagination and associate your business with brands that display similar quality standards. The whole becomes greater than the sum of the parts.

CUSTOMER EXPECTATIONS

Success in your loyalty program comes from knowing what your customers expect from it. Your customers will evaluate your loyalty program based on four factors:

1. Cash value and expenditure required to attain the reward.

2. Redemption choice. Customers want to be able to choose at what point to redeem awards.

3. Aspirational valuation. Customers must be motivated and inspired by rewards.

4. Relevance. The reward must be appropriate, attainable, and accessible.

MORE DATA GATHERING

Besides increasing unit sales and maximizing profitability, your loyalty program gives you the opportunity to collect valuable marketing data that can bring you many competitive advantages. The ability to capture and track customer data from actual transactions is more gold within your four walls. You can analyze, track, and monitor customer behavior with precision, identify your best customer groups, and use the information to target your marketing tactics.

You will learn why some customers defect, and what you can do to bring more of them back.

Finally, you can use the data to construct a profile of your ideal customer.

WHAT WORKS AND WHAT DOESN'T

Establishing a loyalty program is no guarantee of success. Many well known companies have poured enormous sums into loyalty programs and failed. The following case studies shed some light on what does and doesn't work.

WORKS

A recent loyalty program at the TGI Friday's restaurant chain, owned by Dallas-based Carlson Restaurants, was a point-based system. Awards ranged from a free appetizer after spending $125 to a Seven Seas cruise at $25,000. Membership cards were issued at the restaurant. Customers could obtain points updates in the store or via a toll-free number. The program was also promoted on a Web site.

Friday's increased its membership database from 500,000 to 3 million.

DOESN'T WORK

Sometimes a great idea goes wrong, usually because someone didn't think it through. Charthouse Restaurants, owned by Houston-based Landry's, introduced a clever Passport program coupled with a point-based system. Customers received a promotional passport that got stamped each time they visited one of the Charthouse locations. The more locations they visited, the greater the prize value. This allowed Charthouse to collect data on each customer. Members received regular communications through newsletters and point statements; awards ranged from a $25 gift certificate after spending $250 to a vacation cruise after visiting all 60-odd Charthouse restaurants.

Charthouse's program ran into several problems. The perceived value of the cruise was huge—as high as $3,400. Loyal customers with high usage at only one or a few locations complained that they were unable to participate. On top of that, members were loaning passports to friends who traveled to other cities, with instructions to collect stamps.

The failure of a program can be costly and destructive. Don't find yourself in the same boat as Charthouse, which had to backtrack and redesign its loyalty program. Do some soul-searching and careful planning first. Ask yourself who your customers are. Find out what's relevant to them. Discover what will stick out in their minds. Determine why some of them are defecting. Make certain your internal customers understand the role of the loyalty program.

Most important, make sure your expectations are realistic. Loyalty marketing isn't the panacea that will solve all your problems. It will not overcome a price disadvantage or compensate for an inferior product.

Works Twice

One tried-and-true loyalty program is Most Valuable Patron. This one increases awareness and community goodwill, offers an employee incentive, and generates excitement and traffic. First, create a gift certificate for your business—$50, say—for your regular customers, good for 30 days. Then partner with another local merchant for another gift certificate, this one for your employees. (In lieu of the second gift certificate, you can buy tickets to a sporting or other event.)

Give one of each of the certificates to your regular customers. The customer uses your gift certificate at your business and gives the other (or the tickets) to an employee who has provided superior service. This is a great way of marketing simultaneously to your internal and external customers: you reward your regulars while building long-term loyalty on both sides.

Meet Your Neighbor

Customers are not masses of unidentified strangers who wander into your life now and then. Think of them as your neighbors. Get to know them. This is even easier to do with social media these days. You have the ability to get customers to 'like' posts or take little mini surveys for fun. Think up ways to communicate with them and keep the conversation going consistently.

Customers don't lead businesses—they follow where they are led. No customer demanded cellular phones, iPods, or tablet computers. These were developed by aggressive, enterprising companies that analyzed consumer habits, needs and desires, then created products to meet those needs.

The same idea works on a local scale, with your local business. What you must do is lead your customer to co-create your business's future.

Collecting the name, address, email and birth and anniversary dates of all the neighbors who patronize your business will give you the information you need to communicate with them personally and at the appropriate times. Database promotions can boost your sales curve because your present customers are your most profitable ones. You don't have to spend a cent to get them.

Friendship, respect, and belonging aren't created in the course of a few random transactions or conversations either. They happen in long-term relationships. Establish relationships with your neighbors, meet their need for belonging, and you will prosper.

Traditional marketing treats your business like a leaking bucket: you have to keep filling it by traditional marketing methods—advertising—to replace the business that continuously defects to your competitors or brand leaders. By knowing your customers and using effective customer retention techniques, you can plug the leaks and increase your bucket's contents.

STEPS TO BUILDING EXCELLENT CUSTOMER RELATIONSHIPS

1. Provide the unexpected extra. Always give extra value. A surprise discount or special offer, such as a unexpected giveaway on your Facebook page, or some kind of walk-in door prize, can make the difference between a memorable experience and a run-of-the-mill shopping trip.

2. Treat your customers as authorities, as unpaid consultants. Don't be afraid to ask their advice or their opinions about your operation, such as how you might change or improve it to meet their needs.

3. Don't be afraid to reveal inside information, from recipes to marketing ideas. The more your customers understand your business, the more they'll respect what you're trying to do and even want to join in.

4. Finally, take an interest in your neighbors. Look for ways to show that you're aware of them as individuals, not just customers. Genuinely care about their lives and happiness.

OPTIMIZE YOUR BEST PROMOTIONAL MEDIUM

Think of your entire building as your personal promotion and advertising medium—a tight sphere of influence in which you have complete control of the four basic marketing tools within those walls:

1. Your products and services

2. Your employees (internal customers)

3. Your merchandising—a visual and written expression of your business

4. Your customers, through data capture and social media.

Think of the area within the four walls of your business as merchandising zones that stand ready to serve your marketing needs. The zones are plentiful: the entrance, front counter, lobby, waiting area, product and/or service area, the restrooms, and the parking lot. If you run a restaurant, your zones will include the kitchen, dining room, and perhaps the take-out counter or drive-through lane. If you're operating a clothing store or a tailoring shop, your fitting rooms will be another zone. If you're a bookseller, make sure your reading area is comfortable and quiet. And in a theater lobby, a well-directed whiff of popcorn can be a powerful incentive to spend more money.

By using this approach, the neighborhood marketer can highlight the marketing messages clearly and repeatedly, for maximum impact. You can display photos and testimonials of happy customers on your walls, give away dog bones at your drive-through window, and wash people's windshields while they shop in your store. You can also take video of any of these events and post those to show people the fun everyone is having at your store.

You can place posters of upcoming sales and promotions in your entryway. You can give every customer a ticket to a prize drawing that will be held in your business on a special day or night that coincides with a promotion. You can create appealing and interesting displays for the products you want customers to buy. Introduce new items via socials media and post photos of products that can help customer in their everyday lives.

Tactics like these allow you to focus directly on the target audiences that matter the most. Remember: "What the eye sees, the eye buys."

Looking for prospective customers is time-consuming and expensive. It's easier to get your current customers to buy 10 percent more often than to increase a customer base by 10 percent, and you can do it for one-fifth the cost. Focus on getting your customers to come back by making each experience they have in your store a great one.

If you own a restaurant, have special promotions, such as a Valentine's Day Feast for Lovers. Invite your customers to come in to renew their wedding vows, have their photo taken, and enjoy a wonderful dinner.

If you own a toy store, videotape a local Little League game and invite parents and kids to watch the tape.

All these ideas can be modified for use in any retail or hospitality business. There's nothing more effective than covering your own home base, which you have staked out and in which you have proclaimed yourself the village mayor.

Every good fisherman knows the three secrets to catching fish:

- Fish where the fish have been caught before.

- Fish when they've been caught before.

- Fish with bait the fish have taken before.

Forget about all the fish outside your neighborhood. Concentrate on those in your own neighborhood whose business you have the greatest chance of getting. This begins with your current customers, whose repeat business can be turned into a bonanza.

CHAPTER 11

YOUR UNIQUE SELLING EXPERIENCE

*The world makes way for a man who
knows where he is going.*

RALPH WALDO EMERSON

CHAPTER 11

A TRUE STEP-BY-STEP NEIGHBORHOOD MARKETING plan really should begin the day you decide to go into business, or the day you decide to give up on tired, ineffective mass media advertising techniques. But to get you to think creatively about your business, I've deliberately held off on what I consider to be the most important aspect of any business—determining what makes you so special and different that the buying public will choose you over your competitors. This is called your unique selling experience (USE).

Neighborhood marketers create rather than copy. In a world increasingly filled with purveyors of commodities—books, pizza, gasoline, groceries, and so on—how do some businesses stand out, succeed, and thrive? It's not just location. It's not swollen ad budgets. It's not dumb luck. It's not just good customer service or product value. It's something unique. In this chapter, you're going to explore what your uniqueness is and learn how to exploit it.

Everything you've read in this book is about creating a unique atmosphere and market for your business and brand. This unique posture casts a larger-than-life shadow across the path of your competitors, whether they are the big dog in your neighborhood or not. Knowing what your unique posture is gives you a leg up on beating the other guy at his game.

Ask yourself: Why am I ready to wage this marketing battle? It's not simply economics, or to realize a dream, or to fight for a good cause.

To excel in Neighborhood Marketing, you must establish why your business is worth an all-out strategic effort to make it succeed. To reach out effectively to your current and potential customers, you need to believe in your uniqueness. Former Nation's Restaurant News editor Rick Van Warner calls this the concept:

Ah, the "concept," that overused, somewhat vague word we use to describe what a particular operation is all about. We're not referring to the product concept, the service concept, or the design concept; we're referring to the combination of all those things and more that add up to the overall impression conveyed to the customer. Nothing is more elemental in business than the idea or mission that defines a business's reason for being. But we are constantly amazed at the number of operators, big and small, who for a variety of reasons lose sight of their basic concept.

Market position is the essence of Neighborhood Marketing. It identifies your USE, which can also be thought of as what your customer considers your reason for being, and then articulates it in written form. Your clearly written positioning statement must distinguish your business from the rest of the crowd and become the pivotal point from which all business- building efforts begin.

To better understand positioning, imagine being a fly on the wall near your most recently arrived customers, and overhearing them describe all the reasons they chose your business. What you would hear would describe your position, or USE.

Those customer-disclosed reasons are essential to any business strategy. They provide the nucleus for the overall company focus and confirm why you entered the business in the first place.

The unique selling experience must pierce through the confusing clutter and say something so compelling about a brand or product that it motivates the consumer to action, over and over again. Simply to amuse and entertain is not enough.

Your USE must be precise. It must describe your exact position in your market, the clear and compelling promise you make to your customers about the benefit to them delivered by your product through your business.

Here's the key point: You are not in the restaurant, auto, carpet, or airline business. You are in the business of sales. You "manufacture" a variety of products and services. Then you offer them for sale to customers in a display or service area. And to be more precise, as the legendary business thinker and author Peter Drucker has observed, you are in the business of creating, keeping, and delighting customers.

Unlike most retail operations such as department stores, products in the food industry have limited shelf life due to spoilage. There is a greater sense of urgency for selling or moving product. Thus, a restaurant becomes not just a place to eat, but a building designed to accommodate, facilitate, and promote the retail sales of food and beverage to customers through great hospitality.

The same principle applies in every business.

Establishing uniqueness of character for your positioning statement is what so many of us in the marketing arena preach to those who will listen. The temptation is strong to work on the solution without first thinking through the problem. But before you write your positioning statement, think about what is unique in the character of your business. Doing so often raises soul-searching issues that test corporate courage and fundamental beliefs.

ASK YOURSELF THE FOLLOWING QUESTIONS:

1. **What position do we own?** Strip away corporate egos; spend a few dollars for research, if necessary, and look yourself straight in the eye. You must see yourself as others see you.

2. **What position do we want to own?** Confine your position to a workable and reasonable area rather than expanding beyond your capabilities.

3. **Who must we out-gun?** What makes football a difficult game to win is not scoring—it's defining positions and coming to grips with all 11 of them. Crossing the goal is easier when you've X'ed out all the O's on the chalkboard.

4. **Can we afford the position we conceive?** Every dollar counts big in the little guy's wallet. But it takes money to establish and hold a position, and undercapitalization remains the most common reason for all business failures. Spend wisely, but well, by planning an unbeatable marketing effort.

5. How long can we hold our position? Positioning is cumulative; the longer you maintain your original identity, the better your chances of survival. Change tactics, even strategies, but fall back on tested strength. A position won in the marketing war is a distinguished victory, not to be cavalierly cast aside by those whose measure of success or failure is cost alone.

Some classic examples of USE can be found in the arena of product marketing. In the soft-drink industry, Coca-Cola is positioned in the mind of the consumer as "The Real Thing" and "Coke Is It." Coke was the first cola and has indelibly imprinted the image of Coke as the cola in the mind of the consumer. Pepsi, on the other hand, has positioned itself as new and hip: "The Choice of the New Generation" or "Generation Next." Southwest Airlines is in the freedom business, and Ben & Jerry's sells earth-friendly ice cream to the world.

WRITING YOUR POSITIONING STATEMENT

When shaping a positioning statement for your concept, you may want to use the Positioning Statement Worksheet (Form C) and the USE Summary (Form D). The Positioning Statement Worksheet will help you identify your target customers and the benefits you can provide to them. The USE Summary will bring you closer to writing your own positioning statement by helping you answer the vital leverage questions.

The positioning profile will establish a defined, statistical basis for your patronage. This will, in turn, create the significant features for determining your business's position, with the benefits you provide listed in order of priority of importance to the customer. The form also helps you develop the adjectives that will clearly define who you are.

The following sample Positioning Statement was prepared for an outstanding Omaha, Nebraska, restaurant named Johnny's Café:

Johnny's Café is the premier restaurant in Omaha, with the longest tradition for unsurpassed food quality, service excellence, and dining ambiance. Family-run by the Kawas for over 70 years, Johnny's Café is a nostalgic place where you can walk in and immediately feel the warmth and history of a true Omaha steakhouse.

Serving delicious, choice cuts of on-the-premises aged beef in an atmosphere of casual elegance, Johnny's Café continues to enjoy a reputation steeped in tradition, class, and family pride. The broad menu expands beyond its signature beef items to offer home cooked quality meals for a variety of other tastes as well.

An extensive wine list featuring selections carefully chosen by your hosts to best complement your meal is offered tableside, and a loyal staff of helpful servers ensures that your time spent at Johnny's Café is pleasant and satisfying.

Johnny's Café boasts a friendly and comfortable bar/lounge area where beer, wine, and a full range of cocktails are served to patrons waiting for a table in the dining room or just stopping by to enjoy the company and refreshments.

Full banquet facilities and buffet-style catering services are also available for group functions of any size and occasion.

Johnny's Café is an historic landmark that has been happily serving customers since the glory days of the old Omaha stockyards located next door. As the original Omaha steakhouse, it offers a unique and affordable dining experience like no other restaurant in the area. Whether you are in town for a brief visit, looking for a romantic night out, having a business lunch, or just getting together socially with family or friends, you are always made to feel at home in the comfort of this piece of old America.

WHAT'S YOUR BRAND PERSONALITY?

Neighborhood marketers are blessed by individual brand consciousness. They're youthful, hip, even a bit irreverent. They bark a lot and keep jumping up and down for attention. Their personalities are always more memorable than those sitting in corporate boardrooms.

Your brand personality is a corollary to your positioning. It's the portrait of your position as developed in the minds of your customers. It is just as important to develop a brand personality for your business as it is to maintain the brand image you have created.

Maintaining a distinct brand personality is how businesses retain and build customers over a long period of time. Your brand personality captures the feel and the psychological bond you want to establish with your customers. By remaining faithful to the core brand personality in your tactical programs as well, you will solidify your position in the minds of your potential and current customers.

A brand personality statement sets your business apart by identifying how customers feel about you, how you differ, and how your physical surroundings accentuate your personality.

To develop a brand personality, begin by creating a working list using factors such as age, sex, emotional qualities, intelligence, sense of humor, and any other emotionally based characteristics that identify a uniqueness for your business.

If you read the preceding pages about positioning carefully, you may recognize a similarity between the positioning statement for Johnny's Café and the following brand personality statement:

I'm a traditional grandfather who loves to spin tales of days gone by while entertaining folks of all ages. As a host, I'm eager to please and love to pamper my guests with friendly, attentive service and delicious home-cooked meals.

When you enter my home, you will feel like you are stepping back in time, because I treasure South Omaha's past and decorate my house with the baronial elegance of yesteryear. You are always comfortable in one of my high-backed and cushy mahogany chairs and, together with the meal I serve out of my aromatic kitchen, you are sure to feel warm, welcome, and satisfied.

I treat everyone as a member of my family, because that's the only way I've ever known how, and whether you're an old friend or new to the neighborhood—

just visiting or moving in—my door is always open. People frequently tell me that I'm a rare combination of old-world class and down-to-earth charm, but I'm just a fellow who never forgot his heritage, loves good food, and takes pride in making people happy.

When developing your brand personality, you must find inherent drama in your concept—the reasons why people will want to patronize your business. Then, translate the drama into meaningful benefits: a good time, quality service, quality products, comfort, convenience, a pleasurable atmosphere, and value. Finally, state those benefits as if you were describing a real personality—in as many words as you need—to round out the character of your business. In this case, do not make a list.

For your exercise in brand personality writing, you should condense your thoughts into descriptions, then into a short essay of three or four paragraphs.

Once your positioning and brand personality statements are developed, you are ready to move to the action-plan segment of your marketing plan. The action plan will communicate your position and brand personality to your customers.

Beware! Tampering with an established, clearly defined brand personality can be hazardous to your corporate health. Your brand personality is a point of constancy and reliability in a volatile marketplace. As long as your target audience remains the same, there should be no reason to change your brand personality. In fact, it is interesting to see how many established companies, in an effort to regain and retain longtime customers, have recently turned back to ads that call on the nostalgia evoked by their brand personality. A perfect example is Burger King's revitalization of "Have It Your Way."

CHAPTER 12

PLAN YOUR ATTACK

Marketing is an attitude, not a department.

PHIL WEXLER,
AUTHOR AND LECTURER

CHAPTER 12

GOOD NEIGHBORHOOD MARKETING puts your best foot forward. First you identify your strongest attribute—innovation, servicing, pricing, or product quality. Then YOU stake your reputation on making that attribute a continuing part of your marketing communications.

To develop a successful attack, the military mind examines all its field-gathered intelligence, the state of its resources and reserves, its known firepower, the area where the battle will take place, and the hour it will start.

In much the same way, the neighborhood marketer assembles all her key information to determine strengths and weaknesses. Although information gathering is largely the province of a support staff, the neighborhood marketer can benefit from professional assistance when analyzing it.

This chapter is about turning key background information about your business into opportunities that will guide your marketing plan to success.

Identifying Your Areas of Opportunity

Begin your analysis by identifying your strengths and weaknesses. List only those that can be affected by marketing action. Using Forms E1 through E9 in the appendix, list all the strengths on the left side of the page and all weaknesses on the right. Don't trust your memory, and don't swamp yourself with too many lists. Once you've listed all possible marketing-related strengths and weaknesses, rank them according to the following criteria:

1. Urgency. How serious is the weakness? How outstanding is the strength?

2. Achievability. Can the weakness be corrected or the strength exploited through reasonable, economical efforts? This step in the process is the most important and should not be rushed.

Schedule some time over several days to sift through this information, reading through each worksheet and the research data with a careful eye. Think of your documents as photo negatives being prepared for an album. Study everything carefully to bring the data into sharp focus.

Once you've ranked your strengths and weaknesses by applying these criteria realistically, choose the top three or four as your immediate areas of action and reserve the remainder for second-year or third-year planning. Don't bite off more than you can chew! Most of the items at the middle or bottom of your list can wait until more urgent priorities are addressed.

The next step is to draw conclusions about your strengths and weaknesses. This goes beyond identifying them. By probing into the whys and hows, you can turn each strength or weakness into an opportunity. Your conclusions should be interpretations of your data, not statements of fact. They will include the articulation of the strategy you wish to employ to capitalize on the opportunity. Thus, when drawing up a tactical plan of attack, you can include broad strategies within your conclusions in order to focus your marketing effort. We recommend creating a series of marketing conclusions for each segment of your categories.

By this point in the process, you have already been through the hardest part of the Neighborhood Marketing program. If you've done your job well, you'll see marketing opportunities already beginning to take shape.

Before correlating all areas into a comprehensive marketing effort, retrace your steps to the initial reason you opened your business. Are you on track with your original theme? Are your customers today still reacting to your business the way you anticipated?

SEGMENTING YOUR OBJECTIVES

Although your overall objective is to increase top-line sales, you should look at your statistics to determine how you can segment your objectives in terms of specific products or services or, in the case of a restaurant, mealtimes. Suppose, for example,

THERE ARE ONLY FOUR WAYS TO ACHIEVE SALES OBJECTIVES:

1. Increase frequency of current customers.

2. Increase new trial (= new customers).

3. Increase transaction average.

4. Increase party size (in hospitality).

your sales information shows total sales up 13 percent over the previous year but the lunch segment down 5 percent.

Your first reaction might be to focus on improving lunch sales—but that would not be fishing when the fish are biting. The figures tell you that your best sales-building opportunity is during dinner, because that's where your momentum already is.

A Neighborhood Marketer can create an objective for each month, quarter, year, or other period. I recommend one objective per quarter—it's easiest to manage. When developing objectives for your marketing plans, use the Objectives/Strategies/Tactics Worksheet (Form F).

DEVELOPING STRATEGIES

Once your objectives are clearly defined, your next step is to develop a strategy to achieve each of them. Although your strategy may restate the objective, it will invariably extend it by stating a general action to be taken and a customer group toward which that action will be directed.

Make sure a component of your strategy includes a focus on one of these areas. Here's a sample objective, followed by a supporting strategy:

Objective. To increase overall July–December sales by 10 percent

(from $1.0 million in 2004 to $1.1 million in 2005).

Strategy #1. To achieve $60,000 of this increase, we will target current

dinner customers with a frequency-building promotion that

will add $10,000 per month to the top line (1,000 visits at $10 per

visit each month) over six months.

Strategy #2. To achieve the remaining $40,000, we will focus on increasing our check average from $10 to $11 per person. This $1 increase will be achieved by targeting current customers and employees (internal customers) with a series of promotional campaigns that will enhance the dining experience of customers.

As you see, you can adopt more than one strategy for achieving your objective, but with only one focus per strategy. The next step is to identify the most appropriate tactical activities and promotions for the audiences targeted in each of your strategies.

IDENTIFYING THE CORRECT TACTICAL PROMOTIONS

The techniques used in a promotion—what is said to the audience and how it will look and feel—is important to the promotion-planning process. But first you must develop a sound promotional tactic that matches the strategy to the audience you're targeting. To do this, you must know what motivates that audience. Your research data and the following ideas should be considered:

1. Neighborhood Marketing tactics should be exciting, enjoyable experiences for current customers, potential customers, and your internal troops. Therefore, ask them for ideas. They may surprise you!

2. Conduct brainstorming sessions with your creative agency and promotional agency, if you use such services. They should participate with ideas or suggestions that target your strategies.

3. Use previously successful tactical programs. Ideas or promotions that were successful in the past may be customized and tweaked for reuse.

4. Borrow from and customize to your business the many sales-building promotional ideas I've included in this book.

5. Order the latest edition of our 501 Killer Marketing Tactics from Tom Feltenstein's Power Marketing Academy.

Use Form G in the appendix to document your promotion, including your objective, strategies, and tactical programs, all on one page. Important areas on the form include timing, target audience, materials needed, the offer to be made, the steps necessary to undertake the program, and the means of applying the promotional tactic to the target audience.

VERTICAL INTEGRATION OF TACTICS

When planning tactics, remember this: One message, communicated in many different ways, is more effective and less confusing than many different messages communicated in many different ways. No level of marketing should be ignored when choosing the best medium for delivering your message to the targeted audiences.

CHAPTER 13

MERCHANDISE THE ZONE

People spend money when and where they feel good.

WALT DISNEY

CHAPTER 13

ZONE MERCHANDISING IS A POWERFUL marketing technique that divides your store into distinct merchandising zones and uses them as message centers to send signals to your customers. It turns your place of business into a marketing medium of its own, an uncluttered medium that is more effective than radio, television, or print—a medium that you don't have to share with anyone else.

Neighborhood Marketing is the view of your business as a medium: a nearly perfect micro-world where you control every inch of the physical space and everything that occurs inside the four walls, including your current customers. Your fight for the customer's dollar takes place within these four walls and in your neighborhood. Inside your walls, the advantage is yours to use or to lose— but on your own turf, you should have no problem differentiating yourself from the competitors who share your neighborhood in your customers' eyes.

One of the most effective ways to win the battle is to look at the space inside and near those four walls as being made up of marketing zones, from the curb to your employees to the washrooms. Zone merchandising is the planned, purposeful use of the physical areas in and around your place of business to increase sales and revenues by influencing customer perception and buying decisions, using specific promotional messages or visuals in each zone.

Fifty percent of your customers' first impression is made in the first three seconds after they enter your four walls. Those walls speak to your customers whether you know it or not. Make sure the message is one you want them to hear. Don't forget this includes social media. Monitor everything on your website and social media pages the same way you would a physical location. Customers develop impressions from reading old posts so don't leave something there that doesn't suit your new focus.

YOUR INTERNAL-CUSTOMER ZONE

The first step in putting together a winning promotion is to enlist the enthusiasm and commitment of employees. When employees sense caring and commitment from the owners or operators of their business, they become marketing ambassadors who will spread their enthusiasm to customers and create outstanding experiences for them. For a superlative example of this principle, take a trip to Disney World.

To turn employees into dynamic marketing ambassadors, treat your internal customers as partners in your promotions. Involve them in your total marketing effort—not simply by telling them what they should do or how they should do it, but by asking for their input.

There are many proven tactics for generating employee enthusiasm:

- Reward those who participate in inside or outside promotional activities, such as distributing flyers, offering product or service samples, networking, or selling gift certificates.

- Create short-term contests that involve the whole business. When a sales goal is achieved, the entire team should get the benefit in the form of prizes, picnics, drawings, or certificates.

- Offer your employees educational matching funds, classes in checkbook balancing or computers, or referrals to legal or financial planners.

These are but a few possibilities. Choose the ones that matter most to them.

Benefits like these have a positive impact on staff, making them feel more like part of the family. Tactics that focus on increasing sales through employee growth and education are also important facets of promotional successes. Staff members should be rewarded individually for their sales, skills, or developmental achievements.

For more ideas on employee-motivation tactics, buy a copy of my new book, *501 Killer Marketing Tactics*. It has dozens of tactical promotions that target your internal customer to increase employee morale and teamwork.

YOUR CATALOG ZONE

Almost any business can make good use of an attractive piece of sales literature describing its products and prices. Department stores have in-store catalogs that help a customer make buying decisions. Lawyers, chiropractors, and personal trainers can benefit from a brochure showing services and hourly rates. In your restaurant, the menu is your first line of attack because it is such a powerful expression of your marketing effort.

An effectively designed catalog, brochure, or menu will raise your profits and cash flow by persuading customers to select the items or services you most want to sell, such as those with the highest gross profit margins. To a large extent, customers' buying patterns can be engineered by the strategic design and layout of the promotional piece—graphics, format, item presentation, price points, etc.

Invest plenty of thought and energy into your handouts and catalogs, just as we did at George's linen store. If you're selling a beautiful, colorful product, why not use color? It's a proven sales enhancer.

All customers like to read about products and services, as long as you make the information relevant to them. The printed word and the powerful image often say more and are held in higher esteem than all the spoken persuasion in the world.

YOUR PARKING LOT ZONE

Parking is a big issue with most customers. First, make sure your parking area is safe and well lighted. Beyond that, your parking lot is usually the first marketing zone your customer encounters, so you should start your promotions there. It's an opportunity to use marquees, banners, sandwich boards, entrance and exit signs, and music to distinguish yourself from your competition.

If you offer customers valet parking, work with the service to promote courtesy and concern for customers' automobiles. Valets can also be recruited to place flyers, promotional certificates, or air fresheners in cars to keep your business at the top of customers' minds. Washed windows and vacuumed interiors are unexpected delights that can generate powerful goodwill and word-of-mouth for you as well.

YOUR ENTRY ZONE

Your entryway, foyer, or lobby is your first indoor marketing zone, the place where customers come entirely within your marketing influence. There are many tools you can use to promote your business here: posters, ceiling danglers, door decals, community walls, retail and merchandise displays, product samples, and many others. Create an expectation about what the customer will experience.

YOUR FRONT-COUNTER ZONE

When someone walks into your jewelry store, clothing shop, or camera business, what's the first thing she hears? Is it "Do you need help?" If so, you've already blown it. The customer should always be made to feel welcome, not just a person whose arrival has caused an unwelcome break in your routine.

The first interaction between your customer and your employee is at the front counter. You can't avoid it, so don't blow it by asking a lame question you already know the answer to. Make sure the customer sees a smiling face and hears, "How can I help you?" or "That camera you're looking at is one of the best you can buy for that price," or "We have a necklace that will go perfectly with those beautiful earrings!"

In a quick-service food operation, the front counter is not only the point where crew and customer first communicate, it's a good place for register toppers, product boards, counter cards, wall posters, premiums, and point-of-purchase merchandise.

YOUR LOUNGE/WAITING AREA/SALES FLOOR ZONE

The main sales floor or service area of your business should be a comfortable but stimulating place where courteous, friendly relationships and superb service can transform an indifferent customer into a loyal patron. Within this zone are areas where customers may choose or be forced to spend a few minutes—the bar or waiting area of a restaurant, perhaps, or a lunchroom or restroom in a retail store. There are many tools available to enhance your marketing in these areas.

On tables and countertops you can make available flyers promoting your specials, samples of your products, and novelty items that reinforce your image. You can have QR codes embedded in all your materials so customers can go straight to your website or other promotion right from their phone.

One simple but effective and inexpensive marketing tool is a scratch pad with your business's name on it. People keep these because they are useful—and every time a customer writes a note and tears off a sheet, she is marketing you to herself, as well as to the person who gets the note.

Your walls can be decorated with artistic posters befitting your brand and your product. Starbucks, one of the most successful marketers in the world, does little advertising for its stores. But when you walk into a Starbucks, you find comfortable seating, complimentary lighting, a perfectly zoned environment with lush color photos of coffee beans and other coffee-related images on the walls, even today's newspaper. It's all marketing, without a second of air time.

Everything sells....

Even the restrooms become marketing zones with clever use of piped-in music, event posters, and comment chalkboards. An employee checklist for scheduled cleanup shows your customers that the restroom is being tended to. That's why elevator inspections are posted in elevators—people read them! The restroom wall is another good place to promote gift certificates, featured products, or just artwork that reflects the culture of your business.

A small auto repair shop in New Jersey that I know of was owned for years by a collector of oil company toys, oil cans, brochures, and other memorabilia bearing long-forgotten logos. Rather than keeping these at home, the owner built cases and shelves around the walls of his waiting area and put his collection on display—toy trucks, rulers, model service stations, and the like. He had collected hundreds of items; it was like walking into a museum. Customers spent much of their waiting time looking at the collection, and it gave them a sense of family and loyalty with the repair shop and its owner.

Next time you're out shopping or dining, look at everything you see with a different set of eyes. Observe how carefully and meticulously (or how thoughtlessly) every item, every color, every space has been designed to communicate something that represents that business. Now look at your establishment—and ask yourself, What is the message I am sharing?

YOUR OFFICE ZONE

Your office is where you handle customer complaints and train employees. Create a script that will guide staff members at any level to respond to complaints courteously and promptly, in person or over the telephone. This is an excellent way for the neighborhood marketer to enhance customer satisfaction.

This zone is also where you deal with vendors, an important constituency. An effective but often overlooked tactic is to hand your vendors a stack of gift certificates each month to thank them for their relationship with you. Pampered vendors can become not only your best customers but also your best word-of-mouth marketers.

YOUR PRODUCTION ZONE

The "front of the house" is the part of your business that customers routinely see, but don't neglect the "back of the house," whether it is the garage or factory floor, the kitchen, the cutting room, or any space where employees produce, store, or prepare what you sell. Make daily inspections; engage your internal customers; let them know how much you appreciate them. Show them off by providing tours for individuals, or for community organizations that might be interested in joint promotional efforts.

Marketing to your internal customers in this zone should also be fun. How about rewarding them through recognition posters, reward photos, and contest signage? How about placing an unsigned check (written out for the full amount of the reward) in a picture frame and posting it on the wall of the production zone? What a great way to keep the momentum of a contest going—and when the goal is achieved, celebrate with a check signing party!

BATHROOM ZONE

Bathrooms, after internal customers are the most neglected merchandizing zones in a business. To leverage your business or brand, you could include posters with special promotions, testimonials, images that depict your products or benefits of using your products or services. If applicable, you could even place discount coupons in paper towels or toilet paper.

TELEPHONE ZONE

Not only can you load the telephone zones with big points of persuasion, you also have the ability to cater to your customers by providing them with necessary supplies, such as notepaper, pencils, pens with your logo, and fun messages or quotes.

SOCIAL MEDIA ZONE

Fabulous photos, positive content and great promotions for customers can give each of your followers reminders each day of what you have to offer and how wonderful your service or product is. You can use this venue to offer specials, announce contests (and winners) and upload videos that will attract customers. Don't forget your internal customers too. I was on Facebook just today and saw several postings from a local vet clinic that was having an employee appreciation day. They served sodas from the local Sonic Drive In restaurant and then took photos of their happy employees enjoying their drinks. This not only shows that they appreciate their employees, but that they are happy employees and isn't that the kind of place you'd like to take your pup for his or her next checkup? It was also a great cross promotion for the local Sonic Drive In.

CHAPTER 14

CASE STUDIES PLUCK: NOT LUCK

The fish sees the bait, not the hook.

CHINESE PROVERB

Chapter 14

TO SEE HOW FOUR WALLS MARKETING applies to specific situations, review the following case studies of actual internal promotional programming and decide if you could do the same.

Case A: Competition Strengthens the Crew

Author: Quick-Service Restaurant Manager

"Coming on as a new manager, I wanted to have an employee incentive contest to coincide with the current freeze promotion.

"As an incentive to employees, I offered $20 to the one who sold the most chocolate or diet freezes for the current sales month. Each employee was responsible for initialing the sale's receipts from his shift. This category reached 5 percent of total sales for the month, a 500 percent increase over the previous month.

"The winner sold a total of 171 units. Because the contest was extremely close, I took everyone for a Sunday breakfast. Total marketing cost was $32.00, but the overall sales on this increase were $1,058.00. Traditionally, sales on this product would be expected to drop 15 percent after the contest. However, sales partway through the month following the contest month were still at 4.7 percent of total product sales. Thus, we not only created a customer awareness of the product, we built confidence in the employees' sales abilities as well."

Case B: A Simple Thank-You Boosts Sales

Author: Fine Dining Restaurant Manager

"The objective was to increase sales through a thank-you program in several key areas. One of them would involve sending a thank-you postcard to customers. The message was brief: thanking the customer for coming, and offering a complimentary appetizer on his return visit. Cards were hand-signed by me. The offer was valid for 60 days.

"After sending out the cards, we saw an increase in sales of 11 percent during the following month. Current customers redeemed 20 percent of the postcards. Even higher profit was found in the incremental sales, since the customers who used this card spent more than others who dined here during that same month."

CASE C: KEEPING REGULAR CUSTOMERS HAPPY

AUTHOR: MANAGER OF AN ITALIAN RESTAURANT

"The program we developed was intended to increase sales, frequency, and relations with our regular customers.

"To do so, we organized a cardholder program focusing on developing even greater customer loyalty and frequency. We gave cards to customers and invited them to enroll in this program free of charge. The membership was issued by bar or dining servers. The card provided benefits such as a VIP phone number, entitling them to no-wait table seating, birthday/anniversary certificates for a complimentary entrée, selected food and beverage discounts, retail discounts on specialty lines, special discounts at local theaters, and similar perks.

"After one operational year, frequency of current customers increased from 11 percent to 23 percent, and check averages of VIP members were higher than those of nonmembers by an average of 40 cents per check."

Finally, here are a number of tactics, excerpted from our publication, 501 Killer Marketing Tactics, to consider as part of your four walls strategy:

- Raffle a free service or product, or a buffet meal for a large number of people, at $1 a chance. The winner's name is drawn from a jar holding business cards or from signups via social media. The money from the drawing goes to the winning business's charity of choice.

- Beef up customer counts and employee attentiveness by guaranteeing that if service is not forthcoming within a specified time limit, the service or product is free on the next visit.

- Use a "growing" punch card that gives customers a larger reward with each visit instead of having to wait until the card is completed.

- On the anniversary of your business, create product or service brochures or menus with pricing that was in effect the year you opened.

- In the hospitality field, offer a large booth or table for seating singles only, as "get acquainted" dining.

- Employ birthday clubs, gathering name/address/email/birth date details that promise a freebie during the month of the customer's birthday.

- Conduct "Bring a Friend" incentive contests for employees, with prizes for those who chalk up the most new names in a given period.

- Give customers discount "rain checks" on sunny days to encourage bad-weather patronage.

- Have an in-store activity: a caricaturist, a tennis pro, free theft preventive engraving, a animal balloon maker etc., to build business during slow periods of your day or week.

- Give bounce-back coupons that offer special pricing for the next day only.

- Contact manufacturer or supplier representatives for cooperative point-of-purchase display items.

- Offer paper place mats of self-advertisements or offer paid advertising or trade-outs to noncompeting businesses.

- Always have "take with" items (announcements of promotions, parties, holiday specials) to give patrons with each transaction.

- Use special promotions targeting the zodiac signs for each month.

- Mark 1,000th, 10,000th, 100,000th or 1 millionth customer or 'like' with promotions, including advance notice to local press for coverage and interest from online countdown.

CHAPTER 15

CHOOSE WINNING TACTICS

*One hundred organized men can always defeat one
thousand disorganized ones.*

LENIN

CHAPTER 15

THE BEGINNING OF EACH PROMOTION OR TACTIC is a statement of objective—that is, the short- or long-term effect that the tactic is aimed to achieve. Once you have created your marketing plan and chosen your objectives, you should then pick the best tactics.

Below, in alphabetical order, are some of the objectives you might have for conducting a business promotion. After that you'll find 10 steps you should follow before implementing promotional tactics.

PROMOTION OBJECTIVES

Awareness: the first step toward bringing in new customers. The potential customer must know of, or be reminded of, your existence, location, products or services, price range, and what makes you different from everyone else.

Community goodwill: a positive image about your operation in the minds and hearts of the members of your community. No matter how large or small, your operation puts out an image that is a positive or negative reflection on you. When promotions are geared toward community involvement and caring, they show, in turn, your genuine caring and sharing.

Employee incentives: the attitudes and actions of your staff. These make the first, and possibly longest-lasting, impression customers have of your operation. A harmonious, exciting, and pleasant working environment, where individual needs are considered, will keep your operation running smoothly and leave you and your management time to implement other important promotional activities.

Excitement: promotions that make you stand out among the crowd. In hospitality, excitement is the main generator of your long-term success.

Frequency: promotions geared toward establishing your operation as the place to go. Bringing in new customers and keeping the old ones is important, but once you've gained their loyalty, the goal is to keep them coming in as often as possible. Keeping staff committed: promotions designed to help you face slow days, slow meal periods, even slow seasons. Adding new services or products not only keeps your staff engaged, it builds your business during these unavoidable lulls while expanding the community's perception of your services. Perhaps most important, it keeps you from having to lay off employees. The knowledge that you are working to help them keep their jobs will create loyalty and goodwill on the part of your staff.

Image: the perception the public has of your business. Is it a fun place to take the kids? A special-occasion destination? A hangout for students? A place the community can count on for special events? The image you've established in the community should directly affect the promotions you choose. If you want to change your image, choosing the proper promotion can smooth the transition in the eyes of your customers.

Increasing sales: promotions designed to build a higher check and a higher profit gained from any customer patronizing your business through the suggestive selling of add-ons. Many staff incentives are also designed to increase sales.

Mailing/email list: a compilation of the names, street addresses, and e-mail addresses of all customers who walk through your door. The list will be used time and time again to implement a variety of promotional activities. Do everything you can to get it; maintain and update it carefully and continually. Promoting activity during slow periods: promotions designed to get rid of the lulls. Differs from "keeping staff committed" (above) in that it attempts to build your normal and usual business during off times, rather than expand your business's activities and services. It will also, if successful, keep your staff engaged and alert!

Public relations: the most effective and least expensive way of getting your message out to the community. PR is getting the media (radio, television, newspapers, magazines, periodicals) interested enough in what you are doing to tell it to the general public. It takes really great promotions that are chock-full of the perception of community goodwill or substantially different and exciting to get the media interested. Do your best to gain PR, because once you have been noticed for the first time, perhaps during a substantial fundraiser, it becomes easier to get the attention of the press in future promotions.

Stimulating trial: promotions designed to get people to try you out; perfect if you are located in a transient area. Even if your area is not particularly transient, customers who already know about you may not have been motivated to come in. Promotions designed to stimulate trial attempt to offer something special enough to give potential customers the push they need.

Traffic: promotions designed to bring "bodies" into your operation. They may be coming in simply to pick up an entry blank for a contest, but it's likely that some purchases will be made as a result, either immediately or later.

PREPARING FOR PROMOTION

Before implementing any promotional tactics, make sure you have all your ducks in a row by taking the following steps:

- Determine your objective. Is it trial by new customers, more frequency by current customers, higher expenditures per visit, image enhancement, employee productivity, morale, awareness, or a combination of any of the above? What must you accomplish with this promotion? Once you've answered this question, get specific. Identify a specific target. If your objective is trial, what is a reasonable percentage increase to shoot for? Five percent? Ten percent? Fifty percent? If your objective is increased expenditure per customer, what is a reasonable increase, based on your products or service and current pricing? Or, if your objective is employee morale, how much can you reduce employee turnover by running this promotion? The answer will determine what type of tactic you choose for your promotion. Your best estimate of your specific objective will help you customize the tactic you choose and determine your budget range.

- Set your strategy. You know what you want to do. Now, what's the most efficient way to accomplish it? What can you afford? How do you maximize results?

This has nothing to do with the tactic you choose. It has to do with timing, frequency, accomplishing different objectives during different times of the year, capitalizing on local events, seasonal population variations, competitive situations that might call for extra effort at a given time, fluctuations in the cost of your products, labor, real estate, and other factors.

- Zero in on your target. Determine what type of customer your operation attracts—upscale, blue collar, families, singles, ethnic groups, etc. Ideally, the group or groups most attracted to your concept should be those who are dominant in your neighborhood. Once you've zeroed in on your target, review your tactical options and pick the one that you feel would most appeal to and be appropriate for that target. Calculate your payout. If you're spending $100 on your promotion, how many new customers do you need to cover your costs? How many of them must you make repeat customers? By doing your homework, you'll be better able to see how realistic your promotion objectives are and what adjustments in budget or tactic should be made, if any. Measuring payout for objectives such as raising employee morale or improving the image of your business is more difficult, but not impossible. Estimate the cost of training a new employee, or how much traffic an improved image will generate.

- Check the calendar. If your promotion starts tomorrow, you shouldn't be mailing your announcements today. Nor do you want noisemakers delivered after the New Year's Eve party. Leave enough time to accomplish each element of your promotion in a timely fashion, for creating, producing, and implementing. Write out a promotion schedule covering each phase and allow sufficient time for changes and possible delays. Then add extra time, because Murphy's Law is sure to apply. You'll avoid overtime charges and get the most out of every promotion.

- Hone your product/service list. Be sure your offerings are right for your target customers: the right varieties, appeal, pricing, and presentation. Keep track of what is most popular and compare yourself with successful competitors. Survey your customers by questionnaire or one-on-one conversations.

- Polish the brass. Go a step beyond your regular maintenance procedures. Make sure your public spaces are attractive, that every inch of your business is spotless, that any background music is appealing to your audience. Fix fading paint, broken door handles, and any other maintenance flaws.

- Check the logistics. Make sure you can implement the tactic you've selected with minimum difficulty by ensuring that you have the technical know-how, space, and resources to handle the promotion without disrupting customer service or staff efficiency. Practice run throughs are great ways to ensure a smooth operation. Cheerlead. Hold a team meeting of all your employees and explain the objectives, the rationale, the implementation, and the fun of your upcoming promotion. Let employees know what is expected of them and what's in it for them.

- Plan your analysis. By setting specific objectives, you'll have a way to measure your success. Yardsticks include brief customer and employee questionnaires about their reaction to your promotion. Review every aspect, and you'll have the input you need to make your next promotion even more effective.

- Test, test, test. Try minor variations in your promotions, image, copy, timing, and creative materials, and do comparative analyses. Over time you will be able to fine-tune your approach. You're not aiming at hitting the jackpot— you're looking for gradual, steady, incremental growth that builds on itself.

CHAPTER 16

NEIGHBORHOOD TACTIC SUPPORT

You seldom accomplish very much by yourself.
You must get the assistance of others.

HENRY J. KAISER

Chapter 16

IF YOU WANT TO WIN CUSTOMERS AND KEEP THEM, talk to them personally. Let them talk to you. Let them get involved. Give them a piece of the action. Let them get to know you and do things with you. After they've become your customers, show them you appreciate them. Make them your friends for life.

Marketing Tactics by Segment

With the development of effective strategies, your plan will target promotions toward specific types or segments of the businesses and residents in your neighborhood. Your research has already shown you your best sales opportunities. Your analysis has listed the key audiences you wish to target with your message: individuals, families, groups, organizations, businesses, or other community targets.

Community Events

Community events bring people out of their home area and away from their normal spending habits. You can introduce yourself to a wave of newcomers by staging a special event designed to be attractive to a wide range of residents, including those who live and work outside your trading zone.

If your business wants to identify itself more directly with a segment of the community on a periodic basis, it can become the headquarters for a yearly event such as Oktoberfest, or for monthly association meetings. Neighborhood marketers benefit when they provide samples of products or services for public events and celebrations. The long-term gains produced by the positive image you build in the community far outweigh the investment. You introduce your product to new customers without them even visiting you. Remember to distribute flyers, brochures, catalogs, or menus with each sample, giving customers an added reason to visit your place of business.

Get a calendar of your area's community activities and events to determine when a community-oriented program might best fit your neighborhood tactical needs.

GROUP PROMOTIONS

America is a nation of organizations and affinity groups that are constantly looking for places to meet and dine, hold special events, and develop fundraising projects. There are thousands of civic and fraternal groups that may welcome an invitation to your business with the potential of using your facilities on a regular basis.

Even a big, multinational investment bank and brokerage network like Morgan Stanley understands this. When the company opens a new branch, it offers community groups the use of their conference room for meetings.

Focus on selling benefits, just as you do in marketing your products and services. Gather names and addresses of all individuals who attend group functions. Send these individuals thank-you notes and additional promotional materials, inviting them to patronize your business throughout the year.

ORGANIZATIONS/ASSOCIATIONS

Opportunities for gaining new customers are found among those who either work or meet regularly in your trading area. Your research has identified specific groups for targeting neighborhood efforts—senior groups, religious groups, a business club, perhaps even a bowling league.

Consider how best to approach them, and determine the promotions that will appeal to them. One of the following approaches may be useful:

- Contact the group president or council and offer a special incentive to group members directly.

- Offer added value on a regular basis if members present a valid ID or membership card.

- Enter discussions with group officers to determine whether accommodating group events may be in your interest, including special pricing in exchange for free space for monthly meetings or functions.

FUNDRAISING

Many groups offer well-focused promotional opportunities through their fundraising campaigns. Such promotions significantly increase the potential for group business and allow your business to build goodwill. (Use Form H, Fundraiser Opportunities.)

A business can target a new customer trial program in its neighborhood by offering clergy in a nearby church a tie-in program to help raise funds. The business agrees to match a percentage of any customer purchase as a donation. Coupons are printed and given to the church for distribution to parishioners. No sale of coupons is involved.

The promotion is targeted to increase business during a specific period. The program is promoted for about four weeks in church newsletters and through organizational publicity. An employee accepts each coupon and writes on it the amount of the purchase. At program's end, coupons are totaled and a check is presented to the church. This promotion can be adapted for almost any charitable group. Material costs, mostly the printing of coupons and letters of explanation, are minimal.

PARTNER PROMOTIONS

An easy way to build sales is by recruiting new customers from noncompeting businesses and retailers in the community.

First, decide which promotion method you want to use: vendor-allied, joint, or cross-promotion. Once you've decided on the type of promotion, carefully consider who might be your best partners.

A partner promotion should not cheapen or in any way detract from your business's character, reputation, or brand personality. On the contrary, it's an opportunity to enhance it. Choose among the many businesses and retailers that may fit your profile. Not all will be compatible with the customer base you wish to attract. To find the best partners, refer to your listing of traffic generator partnership opportunities (Form I) to select the best one.

There are four key factors to consider when determining the potential of involving any specific business or group in your activity:

1. Size. How many people can you reach? For any given type of program, the more people reached by your promotional message, the better.

2. Communications. Does the group provide enough resources, such as newsletters, bulletin boards, meeting notices, and membership meetings, to communicate your role in the cooperative effort and spread the promotional message?

3. Work force. Are there enough people affiliated with the traffic generator to help spread the work and implement distribution assignments effectively?

4. Image. Is the image of the traffic generator in the community consistent with that of your business, as well as your customers and employees? Make sure that the image matches the profile you want your business to have in its trading area.

Partner promotions are inexpensive but take a lot of time. You may want to involve a trusted senior employee to manage the event with a counterpart from the partner's business.

CROSS-PROMOTION TACTICS

Cross-promoting is a joining of hands between your business and a noncompeting retailer, commonly through displays to encourage sales in both businesses, as we did with George's linen store and a restaurant.

Potential cross-promotion partners include high-customer-count businesses such as gas stations, video stores, department stores, movie houses, and sports arenas. Choose quality operations traditionally respected for their products and service. Businesses should be conveniently located within the same trading zone, preferably no more than a few blocks away.

A cross-promotion partnership will usually involve an equal tradeoff: you distribute a realtor's business card or flyer while the realtor gives newcomers to the community your brochure, menu, or offer, along with a special invitation.

Sell gift certificates at discounted prices to high-end retailers (auto dealers, jewelers, etc.). They will, in turn, reward customers purchasing high-ticket items with a free product or service from your business. In exchange, you let the car dealer park his new car, with signs in the windows, near the entrance of your business.

Consider giving partners free certificates to present to their customers as a reward or incentive. For example, a karate student who achieves a new belt level receives a free meal at your restaurant, a free book in your bookstore, a free cap in your sporting goods store, or a free eye exam in your eyeglass store. This free product not only generates goodwill for you and your partner, it also builds immediate sales, because the student will probably bring someone else and will often purchase additional items. In exchange, the certificates bear the name of the business distributing them.

Joint Promotions

Cosponsor a special event, such as a 10-kilometer race for the community. In the case of a large-scale event, there may be up to a dozen participating cosponsors.

A dual relationship is best for keeping the event manageable and maximizing focus on the partners. Thus, a joint promotion between your business and an athletic shoe store would be ideal for the 10K race, with you furnishing juice stations on race day and the store providing any special gear needed to mark and man the raceway course. Both partners contribute for trophies and prizes, which include racing shoes and a free product or service at your business.

A neighborhood newspaper or hometown weekly can be a cosponsor, with its name prominently displayed on race day. This guarantees media coverage before and after the race.

VENDOR-ALLIED JOINT PROMOTIONS

Splitting advertising costs with a cosponsor, like a major supplier, stretches your promotional budget and creates a friendly image-maker. Beverage companies frequently will share the costs if you agree to display their product prominently enough to increase brand exposure.

Inquire regularly about national cooperative programs in which you can participate with your suppliers and dealers to expand your promotional/ advertising budget, with a little help from above.

Caution: Joint promotions may be best suited to independent retailers. This avoids the potential awkwardness of favoring one nationally known supplier over a competitor.

Your customers and staff members can also be a source of promotional opportunities. People you deal with daily may be members of large groups, or employees of organizations that would be interested in mutually beneficial cooperative programs.

As with all types of partnering promotions, make sure your business and your partner's business are compatible. And don't forget to monitor, track, and evaluate your promotions. This is covered in depth in Chapter 24.

CHAPTER 17

DIVERSITY MARKETING

If you can see in any given situation only what everybody else can see, you can be said to be so much a representative of your culture that you are a victim of it.

S. I. HAYAKAWA, FORMER U.S. SENATOR, HAWAII

CHAPTER 17

THE STATE OF TEXAS ONCE RAN A TOURISM AD campaign, placing it in a widely read African-American–targeted magazine. The ad image featured Anglo cowboys under a headline: "Yee-ha!" As one of the African-American consultants we work with put it: "When I hear 'Yee-ha,' my instinct is to run in the opposite direction."

It's bad enough to ignore such a big segment of the population, but far worse to try reaching it and end up branding yourself as racist or insensitive. There is a huge and growing opportunity in diversity marketing that most businesses have not even begun to tap.

A recent study commissioned by the Pepsi-Cola company concluded that by the year 2020, the number of people we've historically know as minorities in the U.S. will be 40 percent. This, according to Pepsi, is a $2.2 trillion market opportunity that businesses ignore or misunderstand at their peril. And misunderstand it is exactly what many marketers do.

In case you think there aren't enough diversity markets in your neighborhood to make it worth your while, consider that urban youth culture is an important part of this segment and has an enormous impact on pop culture in general. It reaches all youth. Thirteen of the top 14 team athletes are ethnic minorities. Kids buy the shirts and shoes they endorse by the millions, Anglo suburban kids as well as urban kids of color.

Ethnic marketing is nothing more than segmented marketing. This is a segment that is important to you, and you want to be able to approach it in the most feasible and successful ways.

Diversity markets are significantly larger than they were 10 years ago. They have more dollars to spend than they did 10 years ago. But this isn't a monolithic group of people. There are millions in this country who speak Spanish, but the message you send to Puerto Ricans won't necessarily resonate with Mexicans or Cubans or Dominicans. They all have different needs and desires.

Multicultural marketing is basic Marketing 101. In your visual ads, whether it's print, TV, Internet, or radio, you need to show consumers that you're reflecting your customer base. If you show only Anglos in your ads, or only men, or only women, you are telling large groups of customers that they are not important to you, that you don't value them and don't want their business.

Ethnic self-identifiers live in a world that they may see as already excluding them. That's not a message you want to send consumers. You should have diversity in every aspect of your marketing, including inside your own four walls.

You may be surprised to learn that minority household income is now growing faster than Anglo income. This trend will not wait for you to catch up or catch on. It's going to continue to impact our lives.

Latinos and African-Americans are brand-aware and loyal. They buy premium beverages, automobiles, and clothing, so don't focus on cheap.

Latino culture is highly subdivided. It is multinational, comprised of both U.S. and foreign-born individuals, and it's multiracial. The term Hispanic was coined by the U.S. Government Census Bureau to cover all Spanish-speaking people, but you can't speak to all Latinos the same. There are differences between a Mexican and a Cuban that are as wide as between an Anglo and an African-American. In fact, there are roughly 24 subcultures in Hispanic markets.

If you can't tell the difference between a Mexican and a Puerto Rican, you need to learn. You'll need to understand the nuances of Latino culture in New York City, Miami, East Texas, and Los Angeles. New York's Spanish speaking population used to be predominantly Puerto Rican, but now there's a big Dominican population and even a growing Mexican presence.

If you want to reach Latino consumers, you must do so in their own language. You need to understand that family comes first in Latino culture. It's important to understand all this and more when you invite these customers into your business.

Latinos consider it risky to buy brands they aren't familiar with. Anglo customers feel less so. So you need to know how different cultures feel about your brand. Are you Latino-friendly? Are you female-friendly? Does your marketing reflect a variety of people?

African-Americans are very often trendsetters. They are image focused in many ways, and community-driven. But they are also diverse. The Jamaican population, Haitians, and other Caribbean cultures don't identify with African-born Americans and Southern African-Americans.

One of the things restaurateurs forget is that the African American experience with dining out only began in 1963 with the civil rights movement. Before then, "colored" and "white" often couldn't sit together at the dinner table—but we have a whole army of young marketers today who don't remember that fact. So African Americans are especially sensitive to the service they receive. Little things matter, like whether your employees put their change on the counter rather than in their hand.

African-Americans use brands for badge value, such as Nike shoes. Cadillac had the African-American market all to itself for a long time but then lost it to Lexus and Mercedes-Benz. Now they are getting it back with their newest model, the Escalade.

When you're thinking about how to market to diverse cultures, you need to understand the cultural outlets they prefer. Research shows that the top 10 shows watched by African-Americans do not include hits like How I Met Your Mother or Duck Dynasty so it wouldn't make sense to spend advertising dollars there to attract a diverse audience. You've got to be where your customers are.

Diversity marketing can be treacherous if you don't understand the nuances. Tokenism in advertising can offend the ethnic customer. Using your general marketing materials in ethnic markets can also be considered offensive. Although 88 percent of Latinos are bilingual, they overwhelmingly prefer to receive their media in Spanish.

Here's a fascinating fact: You can take a marketing campaign that is specifically designed for the African-American or Latino markets and run it in a general market without losing any of the impact.

Good intentions can go terribly wrong if you don't have an advisor or consultant who understands all the pitfalls. The toy industry has become very good at diversity marketing, coming up with dolls for children that are Anglo, African, Latino, and Asian. Mattel did this with its line of Barbie dolls.

Then Mattel came up with an African-American doll and did a tie-in with Nabisco, with their Oreo line of cookies. They were marketing an African-American doll with little plastic Oreo cookies. This was a huge mistake. Parents were upset. Oreo is a pejorative symbol in African-American culture—"black on the outside, white on the inside."

In cultural marketing you want to use images, faces, music, color, and wording that contain references that resonate with your customers. Make sure there is diversity on your marketing team.

If you're going to commit to diversity marketing, remember these three rules:

1. Make it a priority. Don't dabble. If you're going to try it, do it right.

2. Make no assumptions about your target audience. Don't pretend to be an expert on Latino culture. I encourage you to hire experts to go out and interview consumers in different groups of the population to get some idea, for example, of what Mexicans think in contrast to the attitudes of, say, Puerto Ricans.

3. Match your marketing with your operations. The worst thing you can do is drive diverse markets to your front door only to offend them or turn them off once they're there.

AVOIDING THE PITFALLS

I'll give you more great ideas and insights about diversity marketing, but first you need to understand the extreme dangers of racial profiling, or bigotry, in the retail marketplace. I'm talking about what happens when your employees put your business in jeopardy by either mistreating minority shoppers or even giving the impression of discrimination.

A MANAGEMENT DISASTER

Most people in the restaurant business, and particularly in the African-American community, remember the disaster that befell Denny's Restaurants, a successful chain of 1,700 coffee shops, when two class action lawsuits were brought against the company in the early 1990s. The examples of treatment at the hands of uncaring servers were outrageous and widely reported. They were the result of poor management oversight.

By the time the scandal had played itself out, Denny's had closed a lot of its stores and forked over $54 million in settlements. It had become a laughingstock, and its name became a racial pejorative.

In a similar action, in 1996, Texaco was forced to pay $176 million, the largest amount ever paid to settle a racial discrimination case. Recently Macy's Department Stores was sued and accused of recklessly accusing and arresting customers for shoplifting on the basis of racial profiling.

Even if your neighborhood is not ethnically diverse, minority shoppers are your customers at one point or other. Think about this the next time an African-American customer comes into your store: A recent study by Howard University diversity marketing professor Jerome D. Williams found that 86 percent of African-Americans believe they have been treated differently in retail stores because of their race.

Were they? Maybe, or maybe not. But part of your Neighborhood Marketing plan must always be to do what you can to make people of all cultural backgrounds feel comfortable, respected, and welcomed. Think of it as an opportunity to crush the competition. How much more business would you do if you made it clear to your diversity markets that you are the best show in town for them? You'd stand out, you'd create a firestorm of word-of-mouth advertising, because ethnic markets tend to equate brand loyalty with family loyalty. If Uncle Julio adopts your business as his favorite place to shop, he's going to tell his whole family.

There is a common and gross misperception among retailers that ethnic shoppers are responsible for their inventory shrinkage from shoplifting. In fact, a University of Florida study of 200 top retailers found that employee theft actually accounts for a far greater percentage of loss than shoplifting (44.5 percent versus 32.7 percent). If business operators spent more time caring for their employees, they wouldn't have so much shoplifting.

The good news is that Denny's learned its lesson, and then some. Just six years after those staggering settlements were paid, Fortune magazine rated Denny's parent company, Advantica, as the best place for minorities to work. Nearly half of its 45,000 employees are minorities, and more than a quarter of Denny's restaurants are minority-owned.

Even so, Advantica CEO Jim Adamson admitted that the problem was not solved. "Discrimination is still going to occur at Denny's," he said. "I hire America, and America discriminates, so for me to assume that we're not going to have discrimination take place in the restaurants is naïve."

So Denny's is still working at it. The company has become a leader in diversity training. Some employees are required to take up to 30 days of racial sensitivity classes. Managers and their staff are trained to treat customers and each other with respect.

Every business in America should be, on some level, thinking and acting to recruit diverse staff and buy from diverse vendors. It's commonsense business practice.

When you set out to avoid potential problems, you are engaging in effective Neighborhood Marketing. Build on the opportunities of diversity marketing, and you're using your four walls to build your profits, your brand, and your business.

SAYING IT RIGHT

How tricky diversity marketing can be is illustrated by a slogan adopted by Olive Garden Restaurants while trying to appeal specifically to the family centric Latino market: "When you're here, you're family." This slogan did not have the desired effect.

Olive Garden did some research and learned that the slogan was actually received by Latinos as borderline offensive. The implication that nonfamily could treat them as family wasn't credible. The approach seemed to be trying too hard and was therefore suspicious. So Olive Garden changed the message and put it in Spanish: "Cuando estas aqui, estas en casa,"— "When you're here, you're home." It was a more culturally relevant way of saying the same thing.

Olive Garden spends a lot of money on such research, and you can benefit from its experience. The chain now provides Spanish menus, forms community partnerships with Latino groups, hires Latinos, and goes to a lot of trouble to make culturally diverse customers feel welcome.

EXCUSES, EXCUSES

The business case for diversity marketing is simple: no matter who you are or what you sell, market share is down because of terrorism and our changing economy. It's difficult to understand new opportunities when you're worried about business.

You may have a couple of excuses floating around in your head as you read this, but in the end, they're just excuses.

"My General Market Effort Reaches Them"

It doesn't, I assure you. African-Americans aren't reading, watching, or listening to the media you're advertising or marketing through. But even if they do, they don't relate to the general market media. Your ad in a general market context reflects nothing about them. There's so much clutter and noise out there that, unless you're talking directly to your customers, they can't hear you.

"Minorities Don't Have the Income to Afford My Products and Services"

If that were true, Cadillac and Land Rover would not be aggressively marketing to minority cultures. Minorities are very brand-conscious. They buy brands that are aspirational, that make them feel good. Today they might drive a BMW, but if

Mercedes does a better job of talking to them and extending an invitation, they will quickly move to that brand.

Several years ago you could not get anyone to wear plaid, especially African-Americans. Now, all of a sudden, the kids in the urban market have adopted Burberry. Somebody said Burberry is cool. It's an aspirational brand. It shows status. It shows you've got it going on.

"I Can't Afford to Do Niche Marketing"

Bank of America now sets aside 25 percent of its marketing budget, about $25 million, for diversity marketing. What does it know that you don't? Bank of America knows that population and income growth is fastest among diversity markets. You can't afford not to do diversity niche marketing! It's the fastest-growing market in the country.

ETHNIC TRENDS AND STATISTICS

In the past decade, the Anglo population in America grew 9 percent. The African-American population grew 17 percent, Latino 46 percent, and Asian 55 percent. This makes for a lot of noise in the marketplace.

The buying power of Anglo-Americans in the last few years grew by 80 percent. Compare that with a buying-power increase of 194 percent for Latinos, 191 percent among Asians, and 116 percent among African-Americans.

For every dollar that Anglo-Americans save, African-Americans save 20 cents, Latinos 29 cents, Asians 89 cents. What are they doing with the rest of the money? They're spending it.

If African-Americans made up the population of a single country, they would rank number 10 in the world in terms of gross national product. Latinos would rank 11th.

African-American women make up 6 percent of the total market. They account for 36 percent of the hair and cosmetic market. The tennis shoe market is 20 to 30 percent African-American, but these buyers heavily influence the other 70 percent. Walk around your neighborhood and notice the number of kids with their pants hanging down and their caps reversed. Where do you think they're getting that from? They're getting it from the kids who are buying 20 percent of the Nike tennis shoes.

African-Americans are eight times more likely to buy a BMW, a Mercedes, or an Audi than Anglos. Latinos account for 40 percent of the market for kids' clothes, 20 percent of groceries, 29 percent of telephone service, and 21 percent of all the furniture sold in America.

The gay market is another segment that shares many of the same interests and concerns as other minority groups. Many large companies today are spending huge sums to market to gay men and lesbians in fashion, travel, and other areas of discretionary spending.

OPPORTUNITIES IN DIVERSITY

When minority customers come to your business, they may be scouting brands to see if they want to become brand-loyal. If you advertise and extend the invitation to them, make sure you're ready for them. Some expect to be disappointed much of the time. It's no good to do great advertising if you're not prepared to meet a new market coming into your business.

TRAVEL AND RECREATION

Where are the opportunities? Tourism, rapidly recovering from 9/11, is one of the hottest markets today. The African-American market is the fastest growing segment of the travel business, and the Latino market is second. The minority market represents $90 billion a year in travel and tourism.

Here are some other interesting facts about ethnic preferences in travel and recreation:

- More African-Americans get their travel information online than do Anglos. But pick any hotel brand or travel destination business, and you will usually not find a single person of color on its home page. Imagine having all those potential customers wanting to make reservations on your Web site and not extending an invitation to them.

- When Anglos express interest in an all-inclusive vacation package, they're doing it for convenience. They want to make one phone call and not have to deal with arranging a rental car, air travel, hotel, and so on.

- African-Americans base their choice of travel packages on price value.

- People of other ethnicities have a higher interest in buying timeshares than do Anglos.

Nightlife and entertainment are industries that play a big role in diversity marketing. Eighty-three percent of African-Americans are regular customers in this area, versus 43 percent for Anglos. More people of ethnic minorities are looking for a beach experience than their Anglo counterparts. Sixty-six percent of African-Americans are looking for a theme park experience, versus 43 percent for Anglos. This doesn't mean they want to go to a Disney destination, but it's information you can use if you are marketing a leisure activity to that market segment. If your store or restaurant has a distinctive or identifiable theme, it may be more appealing to African-Americans.

Forget any assumptions and stereotypes you might have. For those who believe that African Americans hate cold weather and don't like skiing, consider this: The largest ski club in America is an African-American ski club. The largest scuba diving club in America is African-American. What's more, learning any new skill is important to African-Americans.

There is a common misperception in the travel and tourism industry that African-American and other minorities like to visit cultural and historical sites related to their ethnicity. Generally this is not the case. African-Americans are not going to Florida to see the underground railroad. They go to Orlando for the same reason as everyone else: to see Mickey Mouse. But while there, they are more likely than Anglos to take a cultural tour or visit a cultural site.

One survey named Florida as the state African-Americans most want to visit; Pennsylvania and Missouri were at the bottom of the list. Only 1 percent of African-Americans surveyed said they wanted to see Missouri. When it found out about this, Missouri hired a savvy diversity marketing company to find a way to make the state an attractive tourist destination. After all, Kansas City is a culturally active metropolis, a jazz and blues hub, and Branson is a busy country-music center.

The marketing company's target markets were cities within driving distance of Missouri. Their precampaign market research told them that only 27 percent of the target market identified Missouri as a destination, as opposed to Chicago, New Orleans, and Atlanta. The perception was that Missouri was just farmland, populated by tobacco-chewing rednecks. Even people in Detroit did not consider Missouri safe for them.

Here's what the agency suggested to Missouri: Since Kansas City and St. Louis are in Missouri, focus your marketing on African-Americans in your own state and show them what a great state it is to visit. Why? Because African-Americans in other states are eight times more likely than their Anglo counterparts to call a friend or relative in Kansas City and ask, "Is it safe to visit?" If the market has not been softened or prepared, the answer is going to be "No, don't come to Missouri. Go to Chicago or Atlanta." Thus, Missouri had to sell its internal market as much as its external market.

The agency targeted the largest African-American-identified radio network in the country, reaching eight million listeners. They put together an exciting and unusual campaign with a radio spot that had jazzy, sexy music and an excellent slogan: "Missouri has a little sumthin'-sumthin' for you." This echoed, without being tasteless, certain popular African- American slang, as in, "A guy who spends money on you on a date expects a little something-something afterwards." The campaign was a big success and generated a lot of free publicity. It cost about $100,000 and generated about $2 million worth of marketing. Stories about the campaign ran every week in African-American newspapers.

In fact, the "sumthin'-sumthin'" song was such a hit that even Anglos were getting into the message. A marketing executive who participated in the campaign told me that he met an Anglo Missourian ("someone you'd identify as a redneck") who told him, "That's a great song. Real bellyrubbin' music."

By the time the campaign was over, the awareness factor of Missouri as a tourist destination had shot up from 27 percent to 92 percent.

FAMILY AND HOSPITALITY

African-Americans and Latinos represent 50 percent of the family reunions held in the country. The Best Western hotel chain wanted to market family reunions to these groups but, finding that their brand was not well known, decided to hire a marketing agency to wrap the warm and friendly "family reunion" concept in the Best Western brand.

The agency's campaign targeted reunion organizers. It arranged family reunion tours to show customers Best Western's properties and to build their trust in the brand. It printed a family-reunion planning guide and placed it in retail outlets in Best Western's target markets.

Best of all, the campaign was built around a cultural universal: at a family reunion, there is always somebody doing something he perhaps shouldn't—and it always seems to be one of the older members of the family. The marketers created a print ad that showed old Uncle Julio waterskiing. The copy said, "You have enough surprises on your family vacation. Stay at Best Western, relax, and we'll take care of your stay while you take care of Uncle Julio."

People at the agency who were Puerto Rican hooted in recognition when they saw the finished ad. They all knew somebody like "Uncle Julio" who always carried on at family reunions. But when the agency copy-tested the ad with Mexicans, they said, "Who the hell is Uncle Julio?" It wasn't a name familiar to Mexicans, and water-skiing did not seem to be a popular sport among that group.

For the African-American market, Best Western portrayed an older woman, "Aunt Hattie," in a state of high agitation. But instead of "You have enough surprises on your family vacation," the ad read, "You have enough drama on your family vacation." The word "drama" resonated strongly in the African-American cultural subconscious. From that one word and that one image, African-American customers knew instantly that Best Western was talking to them and about them.

Best Western's ranking in its category rose from number eight to number four in its target markets.

KEEPING UP WITH THE CHANGES

Diversity is rapidly reshaping the consumer landscape; you don't want your brand to become a dinosaur five or ten years down the road. Culturally diverse market segments are telling you that their lifestyles, values, preferences, and even vacation habits are different. So is their reaction to communications aimed at somebody else. Don't make the mistake of underestimating the size of this potential market. It's here to stay, and it's not going to wait for you. You're going to have to go get it—now.

Try tackling one diverse group at a time, then building on the success and moving on, rather than going after everybody at once. Some brands and products appeal more strongly to Latinos, while others are especially attractive to African-Americans.

HEADS-UP ETHNIC MARKETING

If you want more information about marketing to specific groups, these associations can help you:

- Association of Hispanic Advertising Agencies

- American Association of Advertising Agencies

- Asian American Advertising Federation

CHAPTER 18

POWERFUL PROMOTIONAL MESSAGES

Ninety percent of the battle is what you say and 10 percent is what medium you say it in.

BILL BERNBACH, ADVERTISING EXECUTIVE

CHAPTER 18

A MARKET RESEARCH STUDY I STUMBLED across several years ago reported that 90 percent of people with wallpaper on their walls cannot describe, without looking, a single detail of the pattern. The average American living room has 400 square feet of wallpaper, equal to 190 pages of the The New York Times. Advertising today is like wallpaper, and we tune out all the messages.

Part of the problem is that businesses insist on treating marketing as expenditure rather than what it is: an investment. They invest all their money into opening a retail store or location—the physical plant, the people, the inventory. Then, all of a sudden, it's time to start marketing and inviting customers, but they have too little money left to do it right. As a result, the quality of the advertising they do outside their place of business is poor. It's the same as George's linen store, displaying linens and bedding in a stunning riot of color and sending out a black-and-white catalog to his 25,000-person database.

Most businesspeople are schooled in operations, human resources, and finance, but they've never been taught marketing. So they follow the pack. They advertise on wallpaper that nobody notices or remembers. And they don't know where to go to get the advice and support they need to do it right.

Whether you decide to do your own marketing or hire an agency to help you, there are some rules and guidelines to help you stand out from the background.

All tactical marketing messages should include an incentive. Those that neglect to do this are usually doomed. Your message needs to be clear and concise, and it needs to speak directly to the action you want the customer to take.

PROMOTIONAL OFFERS

A number of weighty decisions go into developing a promotional message. These choices may or may not require special customer action. Offers are by far the most commonly used promotional tool.

FEATURED OR OPEN OFFERS

Feature a single item from your product or service list and offer it for a special price, showing the savings. Be careful not to discount the product too often. Customers tend to become hooked on discounts if your product or service is always offered somewhere in your marketing at the discounted price.

CONTINGENT OFFERS

The contingent offer requires the customer to take some type of action to benefit from special pricing, such as bringing in a coupon, buying a product, and so on. Price discounts are the most common of such incentives. Cost controls are required for any open or contingent offer, especially those that appeal to regular customers. Instead of increasing sales, you can quickly find yourself reducing profit.

A danger inherent in contingent offers is inconsistency. Some businesses use them to lure new customers with outside marketing, but try to obscure the offer inside the four walls. This is unethical, and unfair to regular customers. They will learn about it, feel cheated, and lose confidence in you.

Use, instead, acceptable trade-up tactics, such as offering a customer who purchases a product or service a chance to buy more, or an add-on item, at a favorable price. Over the long haul, contingent promotions are better than open offers because redemption rates and cost controls are more easily tracked.

FREE OFFERS

Of the five most powerful action words in advertising, "free" still rates as the prime attention-getter. The other four are "sex," "today," "here," and "only." (The most enticing advertising message ever devised: "Free Sex Here, Today Only!")

"Free" should be used only to create a consumer trial or retrial of a main or secondary item, or of a new item, during a specified period. To control redemption, coupons should always be used.

Another commonly used free offer is "Buy One, Get One Free." This offer has broad appeal because it normally involves two customers. Although it's costly, you will realize substantial gains on high-profit items and frequency if you provide a bounce-back coupon or some other incentive for the new customer to revisit.

However, use caution: do not make a free offer for a product or service that everyone buys anyway as an add-on, like beverages in the restaurant business. This lacks consumer appeal. Save the buy-one's and other free offers for new-customer trials or gifts to loyal patrons.

PREMIUMS

Customer giveaways are a popular way to increase business and retain customers. Even McDonald's is sometimes mistaken for a Disney collectibles store, and it recently began selling Disney CDs and cassettes. Select your premium offer with care, especially in targeting the audience you want to attract. If it's an adult audience, glasses bearing the emblem of a popular area high school, university, or professional sports team are often sought-after souvenirs, and they accomplish two other objectives: affordability, and a tie-in to the purchase of a high-profit item.

Always tie a premium to a higher-profit item as part of a promotion that encourages frequency. Although you may have a suitable children's or teens' premium, be aware that the younger set have short attention spans, and fads fade. Such premiums are really designed to attract the attention of parents, so that's who they must appeal to.

BUNDLING

Bundling is aimed at building per-transaction totals. It typically means adding side items to a basic purchase, rounding up to a larger purchase. The variety of product or service bundles is endless.

The most important factor in bundling is pricing. A case in point: The neighborhood cafeteria advertises an open offer of adding two vegetables, salad, roll, and dessert to an entrée for a single add-on price. Those complete-dinner cost reductions might attract more diners, but they will hurt your bottom line if they're underpriced.

Focus on absolute profit. To achieve this, the cafeteria might usually charge $3.50 for its corned-beef-and-cabbage entrée, with food and paper costs running 32 percent of that charge, providing a gross profit of $2.38. Offering a meal pack, adding potatoes, salad, a roll, and desserts for $1.00, brings the total price to $4.50. Your food and paper costs can rise to 40 percent, but your gross profit with the meal pack is now $2.70, which ensures a successful promotional item. Remember, you take dollars, not percentages, to the bank.

A corollary caution: Although bundling offers great value and retains customers, product costs vary, and you may need a sliding scale for creating bundles out of a diverse product or service line. The scale should follow differences in pricing among low-end, medium, and high-priced options.

LIMITED-TIME OFFERS

The limited-time offer (LTO) conveys the message that the value is so great the business cannot indefinitely maintain the incentive. The time period is an essential element. As the period gets shorter, the value seems to rise.

For example, an offer "good this weekend only" should be positioned to support a specific part of the weekend, or the sale of certain key products during a specified time of day.

Urgency is the focus. The message must clearly state the terms of the offer and specify a cutoff date. This message is also great for introducing new items.

KNOW YOUR AUDIENCE

The secret to a successful tactical promotion is your ability to present a special benefit to your intended audience. To succeed, you must make the right pitch to the right people. You have to know what motivates them. Talk to your customers. Listen to them. Get to know their dreams, frustrations, and goals, using surveys and other methods that have been explained here. Messages that evolve from an intimate understanding of your audience have pulling power.

Be Specific

Compelling promotions are precise, not watered down with generalities, multiple offers, or messages. You must offer your prospects detailed facts, in quantifiable claims, that are made with a clear focus. Singular messages have impact. Don't deaden the message with wallpaper.

Also avoid institutional promotions with no offer. These are intended solely to cause your name to be remembered. This may work as part of a long-term campaign for a well-known business, but it does not inspire your prospects to take action.

Powerhouse Headlines

The most important element in your promotional piece is its headline or opening. Your message must grab attention immediately. People scan. They give you a split second, and if you get them in that time, they give you a second or two more. If you still have them, they'll read everything you have to say. The headline, or opening, must zero in on the people you need to reach.

Every headline or opening statement should promise your prospects a desirable, powerful, and appealing benefit. If you try hard enough, you can always incorporate the word "new" into your headline or opening. Be creative. Think of an exciting "new" wrinkle you can offer.

Always build your selling promise into your headline. And make that promise as specific, desirable, and advantageous to your prospect as you possibly can.

SELLING THE BENEFITS

The primary purpose of any consumer communication is to sell; and to sell, you must clearly communicate your products' benefits. Your customers want recognizable benefits or advantages; don't bore or distract them with minute details about your business or its employees and owners. When was the last time you were motivated to patronize a company because the owner appeared in an ad and told you his family history? Tell me why your product or service is better or valuable, or offered at a good price.

When selling a new item or service, let your audience know how great the product is or how convenient and speedy your service. These are important benefits, easily understood by busy working professionals.

EMPHASIZE YOUR USE

If you've done your homework and created your USE (see Form D), incorporate those concepts to explain the unique advantage that separates your business from your competitors'. Articulating your USE gives your customers the motivation for doing business with you rather than anyone else.

Many businesses try to be everything to everyone and don't understand why this doesn't give them a unique advantage over their competitors. They've positioned themselves as a commodity and haven't identified their unique attributes. If your lobsters are the best in the marketplace, emphasize lobsters, not Caesar salad!

REVERSE THE RISK

Prospects won't become customers if they perceive a risk in buying your product. Take the risk away from your customers and put it squarely on your shoulders. Instead of just stating, "Satisfaction Guaranteed," tell your customers that you're providing a no-questions-asked, 100 percent money-back guarantee. Tell your audience: "If our mattresses aren't comfortable, we'll give you your money back—no questions asked."

CLOSING THE SALE

Your ad should motivate your prospects to take action now. Tell your customers exactly what they must do right away — "Visit us today" or "Come to dinner tonight." The essence of direct-response advertising is to get prospects to respond directly and immediately to your offer.

CHAPTER 19

21 Immutable Laws of Advertising

I can fix anything your husband can.
And I'll do it now.

NEWSPAPER AD FOR A HANDYMAN SERVICE

CHAPTER 19

I'VE EXPENDED QUITE A FEW WORDS CRITICIZING mass media advertising,

but I'm not against advertising altogether. There are dozens of ways to reach your target audience without paying to shout over the heads of all those people who will never be your customers. In order to do it well and effectively, there are a number of rules and suggestions you should keep in mind. Here are the basic premises.

1. You cannot predetermine what will or will not work in your marketplace. You must put the question to an empirical test and let your market tell you what products, prices, packages, pitches, offers, and guarantees are most and least appealing.

2. When you test one approach against another, they will often produce widely varying results. One ad may produce 10 times the results of another. You'll find this out only if you try different approaches. Using the data-gathering techniques I've discussed, test various premises and run with the winner, not just the ones you personally like. Get rid of your ego and your high opinion of your market knowledge. Let the market tell you what it wants, then deliver it.

3. Never engage in institutional advertising. Every marketing program should pay its way. The only purpose of advertising or marketing is to generate sales. A marketing approach or technique is either profitable or unprofitable, based on results. Unless it's a new, first-time-customer-generating technique, every marketing program should be a profit center. If your current marketing is not measurably profitable on a per-project basis, kill it and move on to the next tactic.

4. You are a salesman or saleswoman, not an entertainer. When crafting ads, commercials, mailing pieces, and sales approaches, seek profits, not applause. Most companies try to be graphically appealing or clever or sophisticated at the expense of results. Vanity is the enemy of success.

5. Advertising is salesmanship. Every marketing technique should employ complete salesmanship and be evaluated like a salesman or saleswoman on a draw against commissions. Is it paying for itself, or is it a drain on cash flow? Everything must justify itself or be replaced. Advertising and marketing are, in fact, highly leveraged forms of multiplied salesmanship. If an individual salesman fails to produce, it costs money, but it's not fatal. Ads, commercials, or sales letters that fail can cost you your business. At best, they cost you the near-certain possibility of more profits.

6. Every aspect of your marketing should be built around offering more service than your competitors. People are fundamentally selfish. They care nothing about your needs or profits. Most marketing and advertising tells the prospect, "Give me the business you've been giving to somebody else," or, in essence, "Let me make the money instead of my competitors."

7. You must educate and inform customers about your product or service: its construction, advantage, warranty, and comparable performance against other brands. Offer prospects the chance to test or try out the product or service at your risk, not theirs.

8. Read and study every mailing piece that comes to your mailbox. Figure out from your own response what works and what doesn't. Mail-order/direct-response advertising is the most critical test of advertising's effectiveness. The cost and results are immediately measurable. It either works and is repeated, or it fails to produce a sufficient profit and is eliminated. Don't spend thousands of dollars on conjecture without any idea whether your ads work or are better or worse than other approaches. Analyze and track results. Note that very few mail-order ads use large type. Good mail-order ads assume readers will forget, so they repeat and summarize and tell you exactly what action to take. But most important, good mail order advertising tells a complete story, overcoming all objections, extolling the benefits, applications, quality, and performance. There is no real difference between inducing a customer to order by mail, from a dealer, by phone, in your shop, or by a sales call. The salesmanship methods are the same.

9. Failure to use headlines or their equivalent is a common mistake. Failure to experiment with one headline against another is foolish. Remember, your offer will interest only certain people. Use the best headline that attracts the most qualified prospects. Never use blind ads, or clever ads with abstract, unrelated, confusing or amusing headlines. No one reads an entire newspaper. You pick out the story that interests you, based on the appeal of its headline. Advertising works the same way.

10. Human nature is immutable. People respond to the same basic appeals they responded to 100 or 1,000 years ago. Products, language, and levels of sophistication evolve, but people still want security, beauty, health, happiness, riches, services, protection, advantage, self-importance, and related benefits.

11. Be specific. Platitudes and generalities are meaningless. When you make specific performance claims, people take this information seriously. "Everything On Sale" means nothing. How about "A 1998 Lincoln that retails for $45,000 and costs the dealer $36,400 wholesale is being offered for $26,900 AND we're throwing in a $1,595 vinyl top and $400 CD player—plus extending the warranty by 36 additional months—FREE!"

12. Every ad must tell a complete story, using as much copy as necessary. Once you get someone's attention with your headline, you should lay every facet, application, or benefit on the table, since this may be your only crack at the prospect. Your ad must be so informative that it doesn't feel like sales or advertising. Readers become engaged with the information you're sharing. When arguing the merits of long versus brief ads with prospective clients, I ask them this telling question: "Let's say that after many attempts, one of your salesmen gets an appointment with an important, busy prospect. This is his one chance. Would you want your salesman to start his presentation and, after 30 seconds, abruptly get up and leave?"

13. Always put the risk or obligation on yourself, not the customer. Make your offer irresistible by offering risk-free trial propositions, generous guarantees, and bonuses. Let the customer know she has nothing to lose and everything to gain by acting.

14. Education is a powerful marketing tool. People are silently begging to be led. When you educate your customers, your profits soar. When you consider a purchase, you're less likely to shell out the money if you have unanswered questions. When a companyteaches, it gains trust. Teach your prospective buyer everything, even a few of the less positive aspects, about your product or service. Be positive, honest, and direct.

15. Tell people what you want them to do. Lead the customer to act. Tell him explicitly how to buy. Every sales call, letter, commercial, and

16. personal contact should (a) give the prospect an education, then (b) take the customer by the hand and tell him how to act. If you're selling an impulse item, or if it's a limited-time offer, tell him to get in touch with you immediately. Don't be abstract. If you deal by phone, tell him to pick up the phone and call a specific number.

17. Marketing is the ultimate financial leverage. Whether an ad or marketing piece generates 10 sales, 100 sales, or 1,000 sales, the cost is the same. If you've gotten 10 sales from an ad that costs $1,000 but you can generate 100 or 1,000 sales from that same ad space, you can dramatically increase your return on investment. Test different headlines, body text, copy, themes, basic propositions, and offers to see which produces the greatest return.

18. Many marketers scorn long, reader-type ads or long, meaty commercials, and opt for short, abstract, clever advertising. But remember, advertising is salesmanship. Would you tell your salesman to make less than a complete and compelling case? Would you tell him not to ask the prospect to buy? Would you instruct him to be flippant or cute? Don't let your advertising fall into this expensive and nonproductive trap.

19. People don't appreciate what you've done for them or will do for them unless you tell them.

20. Only a handful of companies understand the huge advantage a bonus can bring to the sales proposition. By carefully selecting and offering high-perceived-

value but low-cost-to-you bonus products, you can stand head and shoulders above your competitors in value offered. There are many intangible bonuses you can package into your proposition.

21. Turn the tables on the risk factor. The customer is accustomed to bearing the risk; surprise her by bearing it yourself. It pays in first time trials and loyalty. People will buy merchandise with a spotty quality record if they know they can always return it. If you're the first in your field to assume the risk, you gain a big advantage over the other guys. Most businesses veil their guarantees. They make customers ask and squirm. For some foolish reason, they don't trust their customers. If you emphasize the no-risk guarantee and give customers something valuable as a bonus, you've got the makings of a sale, and a repeat customer.

CHAPTER 20

EFFECTIVE COPYWRITING

You can have brilliant ideas, but if you can't get them across, your ideas won't get you anywhere.

LEE IACOCCA, FORMER CHAIRMAN & CEO,
CHRYSLER CORPORATION

CHAPTER 20

IT'S ALWAYS A SHAME WHEN A WELL-THOUGHT-OUT marketing plan lands on paper with a thud. Unless you have special skills or experience in writing ad copy, hire a professional copywriter. You might not be able to afford what you want, but you don't necessarily need to hire a $150-per-hour copywriter to put together a flier or a local newspaper ad. So I've provided here a list of tips, rules, suggestions, and ideas from Tony Policci (see Appendix B for contact information), a copywriting expert who works with me, to guide you through the jungle of words that can help you reach your goals—or torpedo your best efforts.

GAIN YOUR CUSTOMER'S TRUST

Create trust by making your message believable. In our advertising-cluttered world, most consumers have heard and seen it all, and they've had enough. To persuade people to patronize your business, you need to provide them with proof of your claims and offers. Tell your story in such a way that you come across as real people who experience the same needs and expectations they do. Write conversationally, and address the specific need you can fill. If you're selling plumbing services, tell your potential customers that you know exactly how they feel when their toilet overflows or the kitchen faucet springs a leak.

MENTION CREDENTIALS

Make sure to mention any credentials you may have, such as degrees, certifications, or professional relationships with recognizable organizations or individuals. Solicit endorsements and testimonials from people with credentials. If you or your staff are photogenic, include a picture. Mention the length of time you've been in business. How often have you selected a service provider from the Yellow Pages because it was family-owned or had been in business for decades? Being in business in the same location for a long time conveys a message of trustworthiness and reliability. Let your clients get to know you.

KEEP IT DIRECT AND SIMPLE

In writing an advertisement, a mailing piece, or even a handout, be direct and keep the message simple. Make it readable. When you sit down to consume a meal, you don't eat it all in one bite. The same thing is true about reading. A gray river of words with no paragraph breaks is an instant turnoff. Whatever you write, break it up into short, bite-sized paragraphs. Use small subheadlines, bullets, and other devices to break up the visual monotony. Indent all paragraphs. Never, except in a headline and occasionally for emphasis, put your text in all capital letters.

Once you've lured prospects with your compelling headline or opening statement, you must hook them with the meat of your ad. Tell your whole story, but use concise words and brief sentences. Get to the point. You'll lose your audience if you drone on.

Here are some basic rules for creating the body, the message, of your marketing piece:

- In printed materials, use serif character fonts like the one you are reading now. These are typefaces that have fine lines finishing off the main strokes of the characters. Serif fonts are easier to read than sans serif, which are blockish and look like this. However, sans-serif fonts are commonly used on Web sites and for display type such as titles and headings.

- Keep the number of fonts to a minimum. It may be fun to experiment with many different type styles, but it's harder to read and looks more cluttered and chaotic.

- Use italics sparingly. It's all right to emphasize a word or phrase, but overusing italic type is a lot like shouting. After a while, people stop listening.

- Make your font size large enough to be easily read. If you are marketing to an older consumer, this is crucial, and it's something the publishing industry is paying a great deal of attention to these days. Eyes fail as people age. Larger type is becoming standard in many applications. Keep your font size to 10 points at least; 12 is better.

- Try to control the urge to cram into your ad everything you know and everything you want to tell your customer. Leave some white space so your reader can breathe.

- If you use photographs or illustrations, make sure they are crisp, clear, and captioned to explain the connection to your message. Imagery is important. Millions of dollars have been spent by large advertising research companies to determine that one image truly is more powerful at conveying a message than all the words in the world. People remember an image long after they've forgotten the words. Choose your images carefully. Keep them simple, make them clear, and test to see if you can recognize them from a distance.

DESIGNING COUPONS

Coupons come in three basic varieties:

1. 1. An order-now coupon that can be incorporated into an advertisement, offering a free sample or catalog, or soliciting an outright order.

2. A redemption coupon that offers a discount on a product or service to persuade a consumer to visit the store.

3. A discount coupon that requires the customer to spend money in order to get a discount, as in "buy one, get one free." Rules for coupons are as follows:

- Always offer a discount in dollars as opposed to percentage; or, if you mention the percentage, also mention the dollars.

- If you're offering something free, say so in prominent letters in a prominent place.

- Make sure there is an expiration date on the offer. Create a sense of urgency.

- Keep it simple. Avoid offers with convoluted hours and days and conditions for redemption.

- Always guarantee money back. This is a critical mistake many marketers make. Customers will act if they know it's risk-free. For every customer who cheats you, you'll win many who won't and who may become long-term customers.

DIRECT MAIL

Some of the most effective direct-mail campaigns use oversized postcards that consumers don't have to open to be exposed to the offer. But if you decide to enclose your materials in an envelope, make sure the envelope gets opened. The way people sort their mail today is over a trash can. Unless the outside of the envelope says "open me" and gives a compelling reason by stating a clear benefit, it goes directly into the trash.

The mail that makes the first cut typically has a real stamp on it, the recipient's name and address typed or handwritten, and an unfamiliar return address.

A few hints:

- Use real stamps. Metered mail may be more convenient, but it's often a giveaway that the letter is a sales pitch.

- When possible, use unique stamps, purchased from the philatelic section of your post office or ordered online. Often you'll find stamps that resonate with your message. If your offer has to do with sports equipment, see if any sports-related stamps are available that season. The more unusual the stamp, the more likely the recipient will hesitate to throw it away.

- If you're sending too many pieces to have them hand addressed, then use a type style that simulates handwriting. It may create just enough curiosity to cause the recipient to pause and open your letter.

- In many instances it is unnecessary to include the name of your company or your logo on the envelope. Name and address are enough, and the fewer clues you give that a sales pitch lurks inside, the more likely it is that the sales pitch will be seen.

- Consider using customized, stick-on return-address labels, like the ones your grandmother uses when she sends out her Christmas cards. They give the envelope a more intimate, personal look.

- If you're going to use third-class mail, buy bulk-rate stamps instead of using a preprinted indicia.

- You can increase the likelihood that someone will open your envelope if you use priority-mail envelopes from the post office. You can also buy envelopes from specialty vendors that look like priority mail.

- If you're sending out large quantities of mail, consider having the envelopes preprinted with a teaser message on the outside: "Cut your oil bills this winter by up to 50 percent!" Teaser copy can double the response to a mailing.

FLIERS AND HANDOUTS

Fliers are an inexpensive way of getting your message out. Here are some rules about fliers:

- Make sure your headline is powerful and attention-getting.

- Fliers should read like an article, not a billboard. Tell your story. Use pictures.

- Most businesses use fliers to sell their services. Try a different approach by offering free information or samples.

- Offer a guarantee and a deadline. Make the customer feel that this is a no-lose decision.

- Consider paying someone else to distribute your fliers. The cost can be as little as three cents per piece.

GUARANTEES

Your marketing materials should always include the guarantee that eliminates risk. This creates trust and credibility. Decide how much risk you are willing to take if a customer or client is dissatisfied. Replace the product, substitute another product or service, or refund the purchase price. Eliminating risk removes a major stumbling block from customers' willingness to buy.

HEADLINES

David Ogilvy, a legend in the ad business, once said that the headline is the most crucial part of any advertising copy. In the split-second that it takes someone to read your headline, he will decide whether or not to read on. Statistically, only one person out of six will read past the headline. A great headline example is this one, from a recruiting ad written for Hard Rock Café: "It must really suck not to work here."

Study headlines in magazines. See what the big guys are doing; check out what seems to work and what doesn't. Do not use all capitals. Cover only one big idea. Include a bold promise. Make sure the headline stands out from the rest of the ad—it's all that five out of six people are going to read. See the Eight Basic Types of Headlines on the next page.

EIGHT BASIC TYPES OF HEADLINES

1. Direct. The Direct Statement headline is a clear-cut statement about your product or service. It's usually quite short in length and right-tothe- point. There's nothing delicate about it. The most effective direct statement headlines will raise an eyebrow, or drop your mouth open just a bit. They should have some hook that makes your reader take notice of what you've stated.

- The Shocking Truth about Becoming a Business Owner!

- Gentle Dental Care for Pain Sensitive Kids (and Great Big Babies).

- $10,000 Available to You Now. Congratulations! You Have Been Pre- Approved for a (Bank Name) Personal Line of Credit with a $10,000 Limit.

- Discover a Way to Feel Young Forever.

2. Indirect. The purpose of the Indirect headline is to arouse enough curiosity and interest in the reader that they are compelled to read on. You are relying on tempting or teasing your audience enough that they will want to read more. Truthfully, this is VERY tough to accomplish. This kind of headline is usually only effective if it is combined with some other element, like a graphic or a picture that ties in with the headline to convey an entirely clear meaning.

- 100 Bonus Dollars Are Waiting for You at the Finish Line.

- The Best of All Worlds Is Waiting Inside.

- A Very Special Opportunity Has Arrived… AND IT HAS YOUR NAME ON IT.

- It's What Makes this Mom Stand Heads Above the Rest.

3. Command. This one is a direct command, an order as it were, that is designed to get prospects out of their "comfort zones" by a giving a plain suggestion of what they should do now. The command element of these types of headlines begins with a verb. It's a direct call to take a specific type of action. "Do This" "Stop Experiencing That…," "Grab Your Free Ticket…" are a few such examples of command phrases.

- Select a New Wardrobe. Choose from Any of Our 15 Free Designs.

- Enroll Now! Try Any Course For 60 Days IN Your Spare Time.

- Go Mine the Diamonds In Your Own Backyard.

- Join Me and Five Other Top New York Artists for an Evening of "Art for a Great Cause."

4. How To. This style offers the easiest, and often, the most effective approach to headline creation. The method is simple, all you do is begin with the words "how-to," and follow that up with a hard-hitting benefit or a series of benefits. You can also add other elements that tug on the reader's ego or emotions. If you're ever struggling to find a good headline in a hurry, there's no more reliable approach than the "how-to." It is and has been a favorite of the most successful and greatest copywriters for many, many years.

*   How To Drive Millions of Qualified Buyers to Your Web Pages for Pennies a Day!

*   How To Increase Profits by 37% in Less Than 90 Days. Yes Even in This Economy!

*   Discover How To Turn What You Already Know About Your Work, or Personal Interests into a Cash Producing Information Products Empire!

*   How To Have the Best Marriage Imaginable

5. The Reason Why. The Reason Why headline promises to reveal some vital information the reader simply MUST know about. It often begins with a specific number and arouses curiosity. By nature people love to know the answers and hate to be left in the dark on something. This type of headline promises such answers. It's almost a challenge to the reader—to learn these reasons and compare them with his own ideas and beliefs.

*   7 Reasons Why You Should Stop Taking Your Vitamins Today!

*   3 Reasons Our Fourth of July Sale Is The Only Furniture Event You Need To Attend This Year!

*   7 of 53 Reasons Why You'll Be Delighted When You Choose ABC Carpeting Cleaning

*   9 Reasons Why Neighborhood Marketing Beats Mass Media EVERYTIME!

6. Testimonial. Testimonial headlines offer proof from a third party and work very well when the comments you use are from person the reader knows or are different from most other testimonials commonly used. It is composed of the actual words of a satisfied customer or client and that carries a huge benefit of creating instant rapport and increased believability with new prospects.

- "Your Software Is a Vital Addition to My Work. I Couldn't Do My Job Without It."

- "Neighborhood Marketing Is the Best Thing That Ever Happened to Our Business!"

- "I Paid this Copywriting Genius $600,000 in One Year Alone, Because His Writing Made Me $2,000,000. Now You Can Hire Him for Less Than the Cost of Your Daily Coffee!"

- "I Was Desperate to Lose Weight. It Felt Like I Had Tried Everything and Nothing Worked. So, Naturally I Was Skeptical about the "Slim4Ever Program"…But Am I Ever Glad I Ordered It! I Lost 47 Pounds in the First 75 Days and Have Kept It Off Since!"

7. News. People are naturally interested in news because it fascinates us. News that refers to individual preferences, biases, and personal interests, is always worthy of attention from the person it is directed towards. The key in using news headlines is to target the news so the message is seen as critical, must have, and valuable information. You'll see this type of headline used very commonly on press releases.

- Ex-CEO of International Marketing Giant REVEALS Priceless "Trade Secrets" That Have Been Kept Under Wraps for Years!

- Everything Else Has Adapted to the Internet. Now We've Done the Same for Postage to Save You Time and Money!

- REVEALED: The Unspoken Sexual Health Secrets You'll Never Hear from Your Doctor. Your Husband. Your Wife. Or, Heaven Forbid, Your Mother!

- Doctors Baffled by the Newly Discovered Healing Power of Balsamic Vinegar!

8. **The Question.** Question headlines are super effective involvement devices. A question calls for a reaction almost like a reflex from the reader, which automatically involves them in your copy. Questions beg to be answered. The key to using this type of headline is to focus your question clearly on your prospect. Questions that can be directed to a targeted audience are even more effective. This type of headline should get the reader to quickly evaluate his situation or to start to think about his current condition enough to read what else you have to say.

- Which of the Following Four Fears Hold YOU Back the Most?

- Do You Feel Frustrated with the Money You've Been Making?

- Is Your Future Happiness Worth Ten Bucks?

- What Makes Some Companies So Successful at Pleasing Customers?

NEWSPAPER ADS

Businesses routinely complain about the cost and ineffective results they get from newspaper advertising, yet they feel compelled to do it. One problem is that the ads are often boring, make no specific offer, and give the reader no reason to respond. The only people who will respond are those who happen to need your service at that moment.

Ads should look like articles. Use an attention-getting, benefit-driven headline. Say who you are. Fashion your copy to fit the newspaper's style, type size, and column structure. Write the ad like a story. Include a specific call to action.

Provide information about your credibility and experience. Answer the question, Why should I believe you? Use testimonials where possible. Make a big promise. Use before-and-after photographs, pictures of you or your satisfied customers. Give a guarantee. Offer something free. Set a deadline. Remember that people read the newspaper for news and information. Give it to them.

If you have expertise in a field that's not currently being covered in your newspaper, offer to do a column. If you're in a business that has a reputation for scams, offer to do a column on how to avoid being scammed by unscrupulous operators.

ORDER FORMS

Design the order form as if it were the only sales material being used to sell the product. Use a headline. Make the copy exciting. Clearly restate your offer on the order form. Include a strong guarantee. Print the order form on different-colored paper so it stands out.

Your order form should show as much care and attention as your sales letter. It's the last item a customer sees before purchasing. Make it easy.

POSTCARDS

Postcards are effective for getting new customers and clients to call for information, to announce special sales and products, as a thank-you, and as part of a series of mailings. Print on both sides of the postcard. Use headlines. Use images. Picture postcards get read. A larger postcard will stand out, but before you design it, find out the postage rate for oversized postcards.

PRESS RELEASES

The press release can be a powerful yet inexpensive marketing tool that generates free advertising, but it is perhaps the least understood tool and one of the most poorly executed. A press release should be no more than one page. Newspaper newsrooms receive hundreds or thousands of press releases each week, and most end up in the trash.

Use a powerful headline, but avoid the hype you use in an ad. The first paragraph should have all your important information. Be direct and to the point. Don't say how "great" you or your products are, and avoid meaningless hype like "spectacular" and "fantastic." Stick with the facts.

The second paragraph should contain information that establishes your credibility. The rest should have the sales pitch and your contact information. Give the media plenty of time before your dated event; it can take up to four months for print-media articles to appear.

SALES LETTERS

A successful sales letter has a compelling headline and a powerful first sentence that compels people to read on. Write conversationally; it's easier to read. Talk about what is important to your target audience. State the problem and the solution. Never use hype language. Include testimonials to add credibility. Offer a guarantee and an irresistible offer with a deadline.

Tell your customers what your other customers have been saying about you. Include a photograph of yourself or your staff. Create a contest. Include testimonials, using full names for the credits, along with town of residence and any affiliations: "Rev. John Sykes, Smallville Methodist Church." A first name without a last name sounds made up. Put your most powerful testimonials on top.

YELLOW PAGES

Save money by not using bold type. Larger ads get better responses. Do not use the color red; studies show red does not guarantee a better response. Every Yellow Pages ad should have a headline. Make an offer or guarantee.

More Tips for Writing Marketing Copy

Here are some stylistic points to follow:

- Emphasize important words; readers scan ads. Underscore or use bold type or italics to highlight a couple of important points or benefits.

- Make it clear who you are and where you're located. Make sure your name, phone number, and address are clearly visible or easily understood.

- Limit the number of disclaimers, and clearly state your offers so customers easily understand what to do.

- Clearly identify each item being promoted to avoid confusion and customer confrontation. If you offer $1.00 off the Royal Mushroom Burger, make sure your promotional coupon, signage, advertising, letters of explanation, and all other communications carry the same terminology, i.e., "Royal Mushroom Burger," not "our special mushroom burger" or even "Royal Burger." If you offer a freebie, be specific about size and type.

- Clearly state the exact value of the offer and the difference between the regular and special price. Example: "Save $10.00 on your next oil change, reg. $38.79, only $28.79 with this coupon."

- Make sure each offer contains a directional or locator map for your establishment. If multiple locations are involved, every offer must state that it is good at all participating stores.

- Each offer should contain an expiration date, even if it is a year away. If you devise an open-end offer, such as a membership card for patronage perks, state that it is good for one year from date of issue.

- If there are instructions beyond arriving at a given time and date, state the contingencies: "Present coupon upon ordering" or "Tell our service desk upon arriving."

- Avoid double hits. State that the offer is not valid in conjunction with other promotional offers, and only one certificate per customer.

- Use customer testimonials. They mean a lot, and they get the attention of your prospects. Testimonials that come from credible sources can provide powerful action incentives for your audience. Testimonial statements that are specific are far more effective than generic ones. Use testimonials that contain real-world information: "Your staff had me back on the road in under an hour."

CHAPTER 21

DEADLINES AND SUPPLY LINES

Planning makes things possible. It can drive you through ignorance barriers and force you to come to terms with what you don't know.

RICHMOND J. HOCH, CEO, SIGMA RESEARCH

CHAPTER 21

THE FINAL STEP OF YOUR PLANNING PROCESS is to determine your promotional schedule and budget. Your marketing plan will succeed only if properly slotted within realistic time frames and with adequate funding.

THE ULTIMATE COMMUNICATIONS WEAPON

A poorly planned promotional effort can be worse than no program at all. Planning calls for scheduling all marketing activities on a calendar that serves as both a reference for implementation and an instant guide for those affected by the program. By placing the program on a calendar, you will ensure good timing. Overlapping breeds confusion, and momentum is lost when marketing efforts are spread too thin.

You must define your staff's roles in helping develop your promotional activities. Allow sufficient lead time to accomplish the planning necessary for success.

DEVELOPING YOUR CALENDAR

Before plotting your tactics on a calendar, consider the time needed to implement each activity. First, choose the date you want the promotional activity to begin. Place an arrow on the calendar at that point and carry a line through the complete period to the anticipated finish date. Every promotional event should have a critical path, a chronological checklist of assignments allowing enough lead time for its completion. This enables you to determine the action steps needed to accomplish each program.

Because your promotional activities will normally target specific periods of the day or week or month, tactics may overlap but should support the same objective.

In general, tactics should not last longer than six weeks, not including planning or evaluation. The impact of single promotional programs tends to diminish over long periods.

Once you've completed your calendar for the year, check to see if the timing fits naturally into your overall plan. Be on the lookout for unnecessary promotional overlap, underestimated timetables, and potential obstacles that you know from experience may hinder smooth implementation of a given program.

THE MARKETING BUDGET

Create a relationship between your marketing activities and dollar costs. Add up total marketing costs for a given calendar period and plan to take those costs from revenues. The most aggressive school of thought says simply, "Do whatever it takes to get the job done!"

Create a formula that expresses the success or failure of the promotional activity in terms of return on investment (ROI).

If you believe your marketing plan answers every requirement to increase sales by a given percentage, and you are satisfied it represents a reasonable increased sales margin, your promotion may well end up a wash: your sales gain will equal what was spent to achieve it. You may regard a break-even promotion a success, since it created new customer exposure that should yield repeat business.

In this case, you need only wait until the promotional budget has been prepared to determine whether its cost is realistic. You can measure this in three steps:

1. Set up an estimated cost for each promotional activity in each calendarperiod.

2. Determine total sales for the same period.

3. Calculate what percentage of the total sales your ideal plan will require.

Based on previous sales, you will know what percentage gain you must realize to pay for your promotional plan, if that's your primary objective.

THE BREAK-EVEN INVESTMENT

There is a formula for determining the extra sales needed to cover the expenses for a given marketing activity: divide the marketing expenditure by the marketing investment percentage. Find the investment percentage by deducting the anticipated total variable marketing expenses from 100 percent, where each expense is expressed as a percentage of gross sales.

The following example is based on a total investment of $250 in a given marketing activity:

Variable Expenses Calculation

Product Cost = 30%

Additional Labor = 10%

Price Discount = 15%

Supplies Estimate = 2%

Total Variable Expense = 57%

57% subtracted from 100% = 43%

$250 divided by .43 = $581.40

Using this example, you will need to generate $581.40 in extra sales to break even on the $250 investment. (Note: A franchised operation paying royalties and advertising contributions should add such percentages to the list of variables.)

The following table sets forth key information and mathematical formulas that let you quickly determine the break-even point on any planned marketing activity or promotion in three simple steps:

BREAK-EVEN SALES FIGURES

Variable Expense % of Gross	Break-Even Sales Factor	Fixed Investment	Break-Even Sales Factor
35	1.54	$100	154
40	1.67	$100	167
45	1.82	$100	182
50	2.00	$100	200
55	2.22	$100	222
60	2.50	$100	250
65	2.86	$100	286
70	3.33	$100	333
75	4.00	$100	400
80	5.00	$100	500

1. Determine the percentage of each new dollar of revenue that should be attributed to variable expense (column 1).

2. Calculate the proposed dollar amount to be invested in a given marketing activity or promotion (column 3). For purposes of illustration, $100.00 is used as a standard on this table.

3. Multiply the precalculated break-even sales factor (column 2) by column 3 to determine the new sales revenues needed to break even (column 4).

Once you are comfortable with the budgeted expenses versus the sought after sales, you can begin the implementation phase and get the show on the road!

CHAPTER 22

LEVERAGE YOUR BUSINESS WITH EXTERNAL CONSULTANTS

Plumber's Bill

Wear and tear on hammer 35 cents

Knowing where to hit the pipe $250.00

CHAPTER 22

HOW FAR CAN YOU CARRY THE battle alone?

If you create a reliable plan of attack, how can you ensure that your strategies and tactics will be implemented well enough to meet your objectives?

Most business owners know that day-to-day operations, from purchasing to personnel, tend to eat up the available hours, leaving no time for marketing. Many well-thought-out marketing plans go awry due to insufficient time and manpower. Some are handed off to a second-in-command and forgotten.

Promotions that are poorly implemented are of little value, especially if new competition is already making inroads into your territory. The dangers of miscommunication and incomplete execution are many, and you can't afford any of them. If local marketing is too time-consuming for your own effort, you must delegate authority to someone who is reliable, market-savvy, and loyal to your cause.

The work of a creative specialist can help you create and place print or voice-advertising messages where they will count most. We've narrowed the field down to nine categories of outside support. Some professional companies offer one or more of these services and can combine them into a single program. If you're starting a new operation or expanding to new territory, you may be better served by a firm that can package all these services and follow up with research and creative programming.

If your needs are very specific, such as a redesigned menu or catalog or a targeted mailing of a promotional announcement, you may choose to write your own material, using an illustrator for artwork, a printer, and a mailing house to handle your bulk mailing. You will be wise to compare at least three separate support firms before choosing one.

Client-agency relationships need to be nurtured and allowed to grow. Don't expect any agency to know what to do on your behalf until you've given it time to learn the details of your operation. Great clients make great agencies.

MARKETING CONSULTANTS

Many marketing consultants specialize in strategic and Neighborhood Marketing for individual business categories, such as retail clothing or auto parts. These firms offer a variety of services that include both the tools and the strategy to develop your marketing plan.

The primary advantage of using an industry-specific marketing consultant is to tap into existing data that can measure how you compare with industry averages. The consultant can develop a plan to combat competition, expand your customer territory, or expand a successful business concept into new territories.

Marketing consultants can help a business develop its positioning, product or service mix, marketing planning, strategic planning, and Neighborhood Marketing tactics.

There are plenty of marketing consultants in this world. Select one whose primary focus is your industry or your market, and who has a proven track record with real-world, measurable results. Don't feel embarrassed to ask for references from the consultant's past and present clients.

ADVERTISING AGENCIES

The task of an advertising agency is to help you create and communicate your message to your target market as cost-efficiently as possible. Your responsibility is to offer a measurable objective around which an ad campaign can be developed.

Advertising agencies compete intensely for business, especially in metropolitan areas. This can mean great bargains for the neighborhood marketer. Discuss advertising costs and budgeting with several agencies, including "boutique" agencies that pride themselves on lower cost and individualized services.

Large advertising firms often package their services. They offer research, analysis, creative design, media placement, public relations, photography, promotion, and graphic arts. A local agency that offers a similar menu of services may, in fact, be subcontracting them to specialists. There's nothing wrong with this, but be sure your agency is not charging you more for arranging such services.

Depending on the size of your account, the advertising agency will assign an account executive to work with you on developing logistics. This is to make sure your advertising message is timed correctly and that the agency's work back at the shop is kept in tune with your own ideas and your marketing position.

TYPICAL BASIC AGENCY SERVICES

- Creative skills (copy, graphics, illustrations)

- Print campaigns (newspaper/magazine/direct mail programs)

- Photography/TV-spot filming/radio taping

- Media analysis and comparative-rate data/media placement

- Brochures/inserts/fliers

- Ancillary strategies (coupon involvement)

- Direct mail programs/inserts/fliers

- Printing/production/management

PUBLIC RELATIONS AGENCIES

In advertising, you pay not only for creative effort but for media time or space. With public relations, you hope your message will be noticed by the media and that stories about you and what you're doing will be published or broadcast for free.

Although PR is an essential tool in many areas, too many people believe it is primarily a vehicle for obtaining free space in media. It's much more than that. In the first place, there are no guarantees that a PR firm can generate stories about your store in print or on TV. In fact, many clients who contract with a PR firm are disappointed when the media aren't immediately banging on their door. A public relations firm is just what its name implies: a firm that assists you with direct relations with your public or your existing and targeted customers.

Public relations firms can help arrange joint promotions with civic groups, churches, fraternal organizations, and other targeted users of your business. Their business depends on keeping their finger on the pulse of community groups. Through their own clientele and contacts, PR firms can also open new doors for promoting your business—as a meeting place, perhaps, or as a sponsor in a worthwhile civic, school, or other community event.

NINE BASIC AREAS WHERE PR CAN HELP

1. Consumer press contact (news releases, fact sheets, liaison, etc.)

2. Media exposure (interviews, promotional events)

3. Trade press

4. Photography

5. Speechwriting and slide presentations

6. Corporate identity or image programs

7. Community activities

8. Promotional planning and implementation

9. Special reports and publications

PROMOTION SPECIALISTS

In recent years, promotion specialists have opened doors in many cities by offering planning assistance for any kind of event or cause. They know how to structure promotional programs with celebrity appearances or corporate image programs, ranging from 10K runs to holiday lighting awards.

Promotion specialists can provide knowledgeable yet cost-effective help for a single promotional idea, such as a special opening, sweepstakes, liquidation, weekend entertainment program, or special group event. They may also want to know your interest in supplying products or services at major community events or in developing joint promotion opportunities with private or public companies.

GRAPHIC-DESIGN COMPANIES

For the business owner or manager who wants top illustrative work, the graphic-design company can design logos, product brochures, menus, interior décor, exterior displays, signage, point-of-sale cards, tent cards, and other promotional highlighting. Copy (text) is usually secondary, but if you need creative input, a good design firm can often supply a talented writer to add extra punch to print or Web materials.

Graphic-illustration companies are usually headed by art directors or designers from major advertising agencies, professionals whose individuality and creativity have become so well known locally that they are able to market their talents separately. Many now operate out of home offices, using computers that vastly simplify and automate what used to be complex production processes.

If you have your own copy ideas and are willing to put in extra hours to develop your own promotional programming, the only help you need may be that of a top-notch illustrator.

PRINTING COMPANIES

Although most printing companies offer creative services such as typesetting and layout and have graphic artists on staff, it's risky to rely on them to design materials they are going to print for you. Even large print firms don't usually maintain a separate art department. Hire an illustrator or agency to design print materials meant to convey image and gain public attention.

Your major concerns with printers should include selecting and pricing paper, meeting deadlines, and ensuring the quality of the print job. A knowledgeable printing company salesperson should be able to discuss typefaces, layout, printing methods, color costs, folding, binding, deadlines, and delivery schedules.

DIRECT MAIL/FULFILLMENT HOUSES

Most major cities have mailing houses that provide the many services you need when targeting a specialized audience by direct mail or similar fulfillment offers. The best way to reach a targeted market with a single mailing is to use a zip code list; direct mailers maintain computer files for this purpose. They also provide breakouts by age, sex, occupation, or other demographics, with which you can further individualize your mail-outs.

The mailing house plans mailings to comply economically with postal bulk mail regulations. It can supply an indicia, or bulk mailing permit, for your printer to include on a piece intended for large-scale mailing.

Although the mailing house may appear to be the last stop in any promotional program, its lists may help you, at the beginning of your promotion planning, determine how to fine-tune your mailing geographically or demographically.

RESEARCH FIRMS

Young, ambitious, growing companies must do market research; most will need the help of outside professional experts. You can use a research firm in several ways: to provide guidance for your own efforts, to handle certain aspects of your research analysis, or to undertake the entire research project. A good research firm can help answer questions about your business, your customers, and your competition.

Choosing the right research firm can be a daunting task. Beware: There are research amateurs who masquerade as professionals and who can cause you trouble, cost you money, and damage your business. You should entertain proposals from at least three firms to compare values and approaches. You should also learn more about the entire research process yourself.

MEDIA BUYING SERVICES

Media buying services specialize in analyzing, planning, negotiating, and placing your message on radio, television, newspaper, magazines, direct mail, and billboards. These firms are not advertising or marketing agencies, so be prepared to give them solid direction about your target customer.

Most media buying services work on a reduced commission, which means lower cost to you. Major media such as radio and television, as well as some newspapers, billboard companies, and direct mail houses, have a 15 percent agency commission built into their base rates. Most media buying services will at least split the commission with you.

A word of caution: Since media buying services, like advertising agencies, are paid on commission, take extra care in selecting a buying service that has a good reputation for negotiating the lowest possible rates for its clients.

Once you've chosen your allies, you'll need a store-level force to bring the message to people within the four walls, property line, and neighborhood of your business. This is when Lieutenant MAC enters the camp, as you'll see in the next chapter.

CHAPTER 23

KEEP YOUR PLAN ON TRACK WITH LIEUTENANT MAC

*The only way to convert a heathen
is to go into the jungle.*

LANE KIRKLAND,
PRESIDENT, AFL-CIO

CHAPTER 23

MARKETING IS A LONG-TERM, CONSTANT struggle, and great results can be achieved only through the cumulative effect of sustained effort. However, managers are often too preoccupied with weekly sales reports and profit-and-loss worries to think past the most recent marketing campaign. It's a natural side effect of any operations-driven business: you're too busy making the donuts to plan, strategize, and execute a comprehensive Neighborhood Marketing plan.

One of the most difficult tasks is managing the all-important store-level personal selling by staff and management. From the support team down to the staff, communication often takes a circuitous path and, like the childhood game of "Telephone" or "Whispering Down the Lane," results in a garbled message or no message at all.

One way to fill this gap is to find your own Marketing Activities Coordinator, or "Lieutenant MAC"—someone you employ part-time or full-time to administrate, manage, and report to you on your marketing plan and the tactical maneuvering it requires. This person is assigned to keep your carefully conceived plan running as smoothly as it would if you could spend all of your time on marketing alone.

QUALITIES TO LOOK FOR

Your Lieutenant MAC should know your trading area, have marketing experience, exhibit personal maturity, be able to work quickly and without interruption even when other pressing needs occur, and be flexible in keeping the plan on track by adjusting it as needs change. He or she must be available whenever necessary to get the job done, including weekends, holidays, and nights. This person must also have great communication skills, be known in the community, and be active in church, synagogue, school, or charity work. Above all, your Lieutenant MAC must be able to work independently, with little supervision.

If you can find no candidates among your staff or circle of acquaintances, place an advertisement in local publications, including college newspapers and job center newsletters, and fax it to marketing firms.

Your Lieutenant MAC is an ambassador with a structured program of responsibilities. Here is what this individual can do for you:

- Ensure that employees throughout the system receive timely notification of their responsibilities.

- Visit neighborhood retailers, businesses, schools, civic groups, recreational teams, and similar prospects to create promotional partnerships for the business's marketing plan.

- Provide reciprocal arrangements with local partners in copromotional opportunities.

- Help the business owner or operator with budgeting and accountability.

- Ensure development of all four-walls programs, including proper display.

- Implement and monitor staff incentive programs.

- Maintain communications with allied support companies for implementation needs.

- Utilize computer systems to track promotional events daily. Maintain status reports for owner on all programs.

- Coordinate market research programs (Zip Code, Customer Attitude Profile) to ensure accurate and timely completion.

- Track local market trends that might affect existing or new neighborhood relationships, and identify new sources of business.

This position requires clerical support for planning daily and weekly activities, organizing concurrent projects with differing elements, budget reporting, posting bulletin board notices to help promote activities and marketing events, and creating and sustaining positive relationships with neighbors, staff, and management.

On a part-time basis, your Lieutenant MAC should earn an hourly fee on a workweek of 10 to 15 hours, with the schedule to be developed by the owner or operator. A full-time Lieutenant MAC should be paid based on responsibility, with a bonus structure to reward goal achievement.

Your first order of business should be to familiarize your chosen Lieutenant MAC with the details of your marketing plans, including schedules, budgets, objectives, and support operations. Once you've done that, your MAC should be ready to hit the ground running.

GOOD CANDIDATES TO CONSIDER FOR YOUR LIEUTENANT MAC

- *Current manager:* a person who wants to move from management into marketing.

- *Ad agency staff member:* a person your local ad agency, for a fee, could assign to implement your plan.

- *Recent college graduate:* someone with a marketing degree who knows the terminology and can communicate effectively.

- *Shared marketing person:* a full-time professional marketing representative, such as a retiree with a strong marketing background, shared by noncompeting establishments.

- *A retiree:* an ad agency account rep or marketing professional looking for a part-time job.

CHAPTER 24

VALIDATE YOUR VICTORIES

Don't tell me about the labor pains. Show me the baby.

JEANNE ROBERTSON,
HUMORIST

CHAPTER 24

YOU'VE ARRIVED AT THE END OF YOUR battle reconnaissance— after the first skirmish or at the conclusion of an extended campaign. This step is more important to your future success than anything you've implemented in your marketing plan. What you learn about your results will help you fine-tune your next steps, correct missteps, avoid failure, and aim toward success.

Your understanding of your promotional programs comes from constant tracking and evaluation. Remember, if you can't measure it, you can't manage it.

There are three ways you can evaluate and track your own success:

1. Profit analysis (short and long forms)

2. The GRIF method (Growth Rate Impact Factor)

3. Qualitative analysis

PROFIT ANALYSIS

After you've analyzed your sales and trade area profiles, developed your strategy, and identified your tactics, you must determine whether your Neighborhood Marketing program makes business sense. Will it boost profits?

The purpose of any promotion is to increase the bottom line: operating profit less marketing costs. When considering store profit, always translate your calculations into absolute dollar profit, as opposed to percentage. Hard cash, not percentages, pays the rent.

Confronted with unlimited opportunities for Neighborhood Marketing programs, you'll need a profit analysis to select the ones that will give you the best results.

(The ones we present here simply subtract expected costs from expected benefits.) The degree of analysis should be matched to the size of your investment. Decisions about small expenditures, less than $500, may be made with a short-format analysis. Decisions involving larger sums will require more detailed analysis.

SHORT-FORMAT PROFIT ANALYSIS

Whether you use the long or short format, two calculations are essential: your break-even level and your upside potential calculation. "Breakeven" refers to the sales revenue required to cover your marketing expenses. "Upside potential" is your expected profit (sales above breakeven).

Example: Suppose an in-store promotion featuring a specific product will cost you $100 in promotional material. To determine the break-even sales required to cover those costs, divide the cost by the profit margin contribution after product, labor, and other variable costs (costs that go up with added sales effort). Let's say your contribution margin after variable costs is one-third of your selling price: $100 divided by .333 = $300 in additional sales to cover marketing costs.

Here's another way to look at it:

Additional sales = $300

Contribution margin = 33.3%

Contribution dollars (sales x margin) = $100

Marketing expenses = $100

Profit = $0

Another analysis: If the average price of the product you're promoting is $4.00, break-even would require $300 ÷ $4.00 = 75 additional sales.

UPSIDE POTENTIAL

The most accurate measure of your upside potential is past experience with the same or similar promotions. If you don't have enough past experience to measure against, estimate the likely effect of additional sales as a gauge of the promotion's strength. For example, if you plan to run the promotion for three weeks and you expect that an additional 5 percent of your 4,000 weekly customers will purchase the product you're promoting, potential additional products you will sell are calculated as follows:

3 weeks x 4,000 customers/week x 5% = 600 additional sales

Bottom line on the promotion:

1.   Additional sales = $2,400 (600 sales @ $4.00)

2.   Contribution margin = 33.3%

3.   Contribution dollars (sales x margin) = $720.00

4.   Marketing expense = –$100.00

5.   Profit = $620.00

Based on this analysis, you expect to break even, and you estimate a potential profit of $620.

LONG-FORMAT PROFIT ANALYSIS

Analysis may not always be so simple and straightforward, because greater expense means greater exposure to loss. You may wish to do a more thorough analysis. In these circumstances, it is best to follow the five step, long-format analysis.

- Step 1: Establish the time frame. How long will the promotion run? Consider the length of time the novelty is likely to appeal to your customers, as well as the length of time you and your staff are willing to devote extra effort to run the promotion successfully.

- Step 2: Determine new sales/customer potential. This is an educated judgment, but no one knows the market better than you. When considering the promotion of a special deal, keep in mind the following questions: How many of your existing customers will take advantage of the deal, and how many new customers will try your store?

- Step 3: Apply contribution margins. Let's say that after deducting the costs that vary with sales (product cost, labor, packaging, advertising contribution, royalty, etc.), each incremental dollar of new sales contributes one-third, or 33.3 cents, toward fixed costs (rent, depreciation, management, etc.) and profit. For programs that involve discounting, deduct the applicable discount from your contribution margin.

  For example, an existing $3.50 item contributes 33.3 percent or $1.17. That same item with a 10 percent discount would contribute only $0.82. It is important to understand the negative profit impact of discounts: doing so can save you from designing a badly flawed promotion.

- Step 4: Identify the incremental out-of-pocket costs. Include the start-up costs of advertising and promotional materials (such as posters and premiums) as well as the variable cost of additional labor and product giveaways, if any.

- Step 5: Calculate return on investment (ROI). By using Forms J1 through J3, you can see the extra sales that can be expected from promotional efforts, the financial risk of a failed promotion, and the number of customers needed for break-even. Given this information, you're in a position to make a good business decision.

THE GRIF METHOD
(GROWTH RATE IMPACT FACTOR)

Excitement, enthusiasm, and anticipation often contribute added impact to a Neighborhood Marketing plan. This enthusiasm should carry over to the evaluation of each program. Otherwise it's a tedious and painstaking process.

The payoff for a well-done evaluation may be found in answers to the following questions:

- Did the promotion reach its stated objective?

- Was the promotion cost-efficient?

- Should the promotion be repeated, modified, or scrapped?

- Were average transaction and customer counts affected by the promotion?

You can't evaluate by pure gut feel: "We seemed to be busier." The results of every promotional activity must be quantified to mean anything or be useful. The formula for measuring the relative success of marketing activities is called the growth rate impact factor (GRIF).

The GRIF formula tells you the activity's impact on your business. The indicator is not absolute, since other external and internal factors are also considered. But GRIF is the ideal starting point. We talked about this in an earlier chapter, but here is some more detail to help you understand and implement the concept.

You will examine your data against pre-promotion trends and against results after the activity: pre-period data and post-period data. Pre-period is the time just before the promotion period itself; post-period is the time immediately after the promotion ends. All three periods (pre-, promotion, and post-) must be the same length in days or weeks.

For instance, if your promotion lasts four weeks, then the pre- and post-measurement periods must also be four weeks long. To minimize the distorting effect of seasonal trends, compare each period's results to the previous year's data, identifying a percentage change from one year to the next. Use Forms K1 through K3 to track and evaluate monthly and yearly sales histories.

Two notes of caution are called for: First, the evaluations determine only immediate return and do not account for future payback, which is more important for meeting long-term objectives. Second, the situation is sometimes uncontrollable, easily rendering the evaluation invalid. Examples of factors out of your control are extraordinary weather conditions (if you sell ice cream during a freak hot spell, your results will be skewed), competitive advertising and promotion (the other guy launches a promotion in the middle of yours), and abrupt changes in the local economy (the principal employer in your town closes its factory). These you measure using our next tool, qualitative analysis.

QUALITATIVE ANALYSIS

Once profit analysis and GRIF have been applied, it's time for the final evaluation mechanism. Qualitative analysis incorporates human and nonfinancial feedback. Managers are asked to openly describe their feelings and opinions about the success or failure of the promotional program. (Use Forms L1 and L2 in Appendix A.)

Qualitative analysis measures the immeasurable. Ask yourself questions such as these:

- Did that snowstorm during the promotional period keep customers at home?

- Was staff morale low, and if so, how did this affect customers?

- Were my customers so fed up with traffic problems related to road construction that they opted to go elsewhere?

Knowing the answers can help explain why the program did or didn't succeed. This human factor gives you and your management team an opportunity to record personal opinions and feelings about a program.

Qualitative analysis is essential to the tracking and evaluation of a program because its findings are often intuitive, although they are measurable to a degree by using your internal- and external-customer surveys. The feedback balances the scores and ratings of the quantitative analysis.

Form L2 in Appendix A should be used as your template for qualitatively evaluating each program. It is designed to record your opinion of the program, along with any positives and negatives. You should attach supporting materials (ads, door knobbers, point-of-purchase, direct mail, etc.) that may contribute to the explanation.

Ready, Go, Set

Some of the best-laid plans go wrong for reasons that break a marketer's heart. One of my past clients was a local unit of a major chain restaurant. We designed a "buy one, get one free" promotion to combat sluggish sales and scheduled it for a summer holiday weekend that was likely to be busy anyway. The promotion was heavily supported by TV and newspaper advertising.

When the first returns came in, things looked good: sales and traffic were up. However, profits were nonexistent. The whole exercise proved futile at the bottom line.

Unit managers reported the bad news underlying those sales traffic increases: deplorable operational crunches. Crowds were lined up, waiting, waiting, and waiting. A scramble to bring in more help failed because the product was compromised by rushing delivery. The whole experience was tarnished by poor service that had lasting, negative effects among both customers and crew.

It was a painful experience, but one from which to learn. Had good communication been established between managers and the marketing group, managers would have had a chance to warn of possible understaffing.

CHAPTER 25

MARKETING COMMANDMENTS

In the factory, we make cosmetics.
In my stores, we sell hope.

**CHARLES REVSON, FOUNDER,
REVLON COSMETICS**

CHAPTER 25

MARKETING STRATEGIES BASED ON MASS thinking are dead or dying. We are entering a new world of marketing based on time-tested principles of community, neighborhood, ethics, and caring about people. Look for refreshing new ways to reach your customers.

As Peter Georgescu, Chairman and CEO of Young & Rubicam, has observed: "Marketing will be all about getting brands and customers together in a relationship that's healthy and productive for both parties."

It will be accomplished by:

- Becoming totally knowledgeable about the strengths and weaknesses of media throughout your neighborhood target areas. Every neighborhood marketer should have a working knowledge of every advertising vehicle in his territory.

- Interacting with your customers using the media you choose, so you can measure the cost effectiveness of your advertising purchases.

- Using creative promotions, new products, and innovative sales strategies such as e-mail newsletters to reach your target audience.

- Using multiple communications to reach customers, not just the Internet, or counting on a revenue spike caused by selling 29-cent burgers on Wednesdays.

- Finding a way to measure every promotion you attempt. It's the only way to gauge its effectiveness with customer counts and to test media strength.

Your business's products and services, courteous staff, cleanliness of surroundings, the great value you provide in your pricing structure for the quality you serve—these are the traditional and basic features that sell your customer.

You've heard it a thousand times: The best advertising of all is word of mouth. You've envied businesses about whom it is said, "They're so good, they don't have to advertise."

If you're doing your job, you should never have to spend a penny on advertising.

16 Marketing Truths to Remember

1. The market constantly changes as new families, prospects, and lifestyles reshape the marketplace. When you stop marketing, you miss evolving opportunities and stop being part of the process. You're no longer a player in the game.

2. 2. People forget fast. They're buried under an avalanche of messages, an estimated 4,000 daily. Tests of consumer recall of a 13-week ad campaign found that at the end of the campaign 63 percent of those surveyed remembered the advertising. A month later, 32 percent recalled it. Two weeks after that, the figure was down to 21 percent: four out of five had completely forgotten.

3. Your competition isn't giving up. People will spend money to make purchases. If they are not aware that you are selling, they'll spend elsewhere.

4. Marketing your business strengthens your identity. When you quit, you shortchange your reputation, your perceived reliability, and the confidence people have in you. Even when economic conditions turn downward, smart companies continue to advertise. The bond of communication is too precious to break capriciously. When times are good, advertise because you can. When times are bad, advertise because you must.

5. Marketing yourself is essential to survival and growth. With few exceptions, people won't know you're there if you don't get the word out.

6. Marketing ensures that you keep repeat customers, who may be the key to your referral business. They can forget you, too.

7. Marketing maintains morale. It uplifts employees who see the extra efforts you implement to keep your name in front of the public. The corollary: a cutback in marketing can signal failure to those who actively follow your communications. How many oncefamous Hollywood actors have been told, "I thought you were dead!"

8. Marketing gives you the advantage when your competitors fail to advertise. A troubled economy can force competitors to stop marketing and give you a chance to move ahead and attract their customers.

9. Marketing allows your business to keep operating. You still have overhead: telephone, Yellow Pages, rent, equipment, payroll. Marketing creates the air that overhead breathes.

10. Marketing protects your investment. If you stop, the money you've already spent for advertising is lost as consumer awareness dwindles. You may be able to buy back a lost audience, but you'll have to start from scratch and spend that money all over again.

11. Marketing is serious business, and, increasingly, serious business is about marketing.

12. Market locally. You have to give all your customers something that appeals to them personally to be number one. Nationally, you must first be number one in each trading area.

13. Don't be blinded by visible demand. Preference is perishable. Keep selling the sold.

14. Make sure everyone in your organization understands the strategy, the destination, and the business objectives. Then let them execute. If they don't execute, they get executed.

15. Work with passion and have a sense of urgency. It's a heck of a lot of fun.

16. Stop cutting prices. The sale that cost you a dime to get three years ago, now costs a quarter. And still, all you are getting is rented volume that is going away as soon as you stop paying for it.

FINAL WORD

A lot of what I'm suggesting in my book may seem like just obvious common sense. But when you start to implement them in the marketing world, where the traditional standards have been mystery and magic, you are going to be considered a revolutionary. So be prepared, and keep your sense of humor when people start poking fun at you because you refuse to engage in mass media marketing. Convincing customers to buy your products is the only reason a marketer is in business and the only reason that a company should spend any money at all on marketing.

APPENDIX A

The following forms are designed to help your business from a marketing perspective. Feel free to make copies for your own use. Also visit www.tomfeltenstein. com and download additional forms as well as other information that is updated regularly.

Form A: Mystery Shopper Research Evaluation

Date	Store name				
Day of the week	Location/unit number				

Pre-visit	Excellent	Very Good	Good	Fair	Poor
Call was answered promptly					
Employee was friendly and attentive					
Gave clear directions					

Comments:

Store visit	Start time	End time	Weather	No. of Employees	No. of Customers
Employees' names					

Comments:

Exterior	Excellent	Very Good	Good	Fair	Poor
Parking lot cleanliness					
Sidewalk cleanliness					
Window cleanliness					
Working order of outside signs					
Window displays					

Comments:

Internal Displays	Excellent	Very Good	Good	Fair	Poor
Graphics and signs were in good condition					
Merchandise was neat and orderly					
Store was clean and free of debris					

Comments:

Form A: Mystery Shopper Research Evaluation, continued

Date				
Day of the week				
Store name				
Location/unit number				

Cashwrap/Counter	Excellent	Very Good	Good	Fair	Poor
Neatness of area					
Efficiency of staff					

Comments:

Staff Appearance	Excellent	Very Good	Good	Fair	Poor
Manager					
Floor staff					
Support staff					

Comments:

Staff Performance	Excellent	Very Good	Good	Fair	Poor
Greeting was prompt and welcoming					
Staff made eye contact					
Staff were friendly					
Staff were knowledgeable					
Your needs were explored					
Staff mentioned value-added service					
Staff mentioned current promotions					
Staff made additional product suggestions					
Staff thanked you and invited you to return					
All customers were waited on					

Comments:

Enter any additional comments or observations:

Form B1: Competitive-Evaluation Form

Name of respondent _____

Title of respondent _____

Business name _____

Business location _____

Date shopped _____

	Excellent	Very Good	Good	Fair	Poor
Location convenience					
Location visibility					
Product variety					
Product depth					
Product stock levels					
Service offerings					
Pricing					
Merchandise presentation					
Signage and graphics					
Lighting					
Cleanliness					
Staff availability					
Staff friendliness					
Staff knowledge					
Checkout process					
Promotional activity					
Loyalty programs					
Awareness					
Image					
Atmosphere					

Form B2: Competitive-Activity Record

This sheet will help you track your competitors' promotional activities. To make best use of this form and the data gathered, you need to walk by your most direct competitors, make notes on the marketing activities or promotions they are running, and make a rough estimate of whether the number of people in them has increased, decreased, or remained the same over time.

Location _____

Competitor (name of business)	Date (start and stop dates of promotions)	Marketing activity (description of promotion/offer)	Comments (increase, decrease, or no change in numbers)

Form B3: Competition Survey Worksheet

Market:_____

Location: _____

These are the businesses that compete for your customers. Describe each competitor and its approximate distance from you; rate its threat level (0 = no threat at all, 1 = mild threat, 2 = moderate threat, 3 = serious threat).

Competitor	Distance to my location	How it competes with my business	Threat level

Form C: Positioning Statement Worksheet

Make as many copies of these forms as you need. Use them as worksheets in developing your current marketing plan. Complete one set of forms for each outlet or location.

1. Customer profile (indicate who your customers are by time of day and day of week):

Time	Time
Weekday	Weekday
Area visitors (%)	Area visitors (%)
Local residents (%)	Local residents (%)
Made a purchase (%)	Made a purchase (%)
Age range	Age range
Gender (%) ____ male ____ female	Gender (%) ____ male ____ female
Time	Time
Weekday	Weekday
Area visitors (%)	Area visitors (%)
Local residents (%)	Local residents (%)
Made a purchase (%)	Made a purchase (%)
Age range	Age range
Gender (%) ____ male ____ female	Gender (%) ____ male ____ female
Time	Time
Weekday	Weekday
Area visitors (%)	Area visitors (%)
Local residents (%)	Local residents (%)
Made a purchase (%)	Made a purchase (%)
Age range	Age range
Gender (%) ____ male ____ female	Gender (%) ____ male ____ female

Form C: Positioning Statement Worksheet, continued

Time	Time
Weekday	Weekday
Area visitors (%)	Area visitors (%)
Local residents (%)	Local residents (%)
Made a purchase (%)	Made a purchase (%)
Age range	Age range
Gender (%) ____ male ____ female	Gender (%) ____ male ____ female

2. List the customer benefits you provide in absolute terms (regardless of the competition):

_____

_____

_____

_____

_____

_____

_____

3. List the customer benefits you provide relative to the competition:

_____

_____

_____

_____

_____

_____

_____

Form C: Positioning Statement Worksheet, continued

4. List the benefits by priority to the customer:

a. _____   f. _____

b. _____   g. _____

c. _____   h. _____

d. _____   i. _____

e. _____   j. _____

5. List any other attributes that you want to convey to the customer:

_____

_____

_____

_____

_____

_____

Form D: Unique Selling Experience (USE) Summary

1. What is your target market? Who exactly are your customers?

_____

_____

_____

_____

_____

_____

2. What are the three most important results your customer is seeking from the purchase of your product?

1. _____

2. _____

3. _____

3. List three specific reasons why your best customers do business with you rather than a competitor.

1. _____

2. _____

3. _____

4. List three specific reasons why you do business with certain professionals or businesses rather than others.

1. _____

2. _____

3. _____

Form D: Unique Selling Experience (USE) Summary, continued

5. Describe your target market and their main problem by completing the following sentence:

Do you know how.... _____

_____

_____

_____

_____

_____

6. Complete this sentence with an explanation of how you will uniquely solve that problem.

Well, what I do is... _____

_____

_____

_____

_____

_____

7. Now distill the information from #5 and #6 into a concise statement that represents your unique selling proposition.

_____

_____

_____

_____

Form D: Unique Selling Experience (USE) Summary, continued

8. (Optional) If possible, further condense the statement in #7 to a brief slogan suitable for business cards or stationery.

_____

_____

_____

_____

_____

Form E1: Internal-Customer Profile

Strengths and Weaknesses

Ask your employees for their opinions on the strengths and weaknesses of your establishment. List them, then tabulate them. This short list will show you where your promotional dollars should be spent.

Strengths	Weaknesses

Marketing Conclusions

_____

_____

_____

_____

_____

Form E2: Product/Service Profile

Strengths and Weaknesses

Strengths	Weaknesses

Marketing Conclusions

_____

_____

_____

_____

_____

Form E3: Marketing History Profile

Strengths and Weaknesses

Strengths	Weaknesses

Marketing Conclusions

_____

_____

_____

_____

_____

Form E4: Historical Sales Profile

Strengths and Weaknesses

Strengths	Weaknesses

Marketing Conclusions

_____

_____

_____

_____

_____

Form E5: Customer Attitude Profile

Strengths and Weaknesses

Ask your customers for their opinions on the strengths and weaknesses of your establishment. List them, then tabulate them. Once you've read the book, this short list will show you where your promotional dollars should be spent.

Strengths	Weaknesses

Marketing Conclusions

_____

_____

_____

_____

_____

Form E6: Trade Area/Demographic Profile

Strengths and Weaknesses

Strengths	Weaknesses

Marketing Conclusions

_____

_____

_____

_____

_____

Form E7: Zip Code Profile

Strengths and Weaknesses

Are there any patterns that show up in your zip code data-tracking studies? Identify the strengths and weaknesses for those results, and jot down a few ideas or marketing conclusions. Remember to build and capitalize on your strengths. Resist the temptation to invest all your resources in trying to overcome your weaknesses.

Strengths	Weaknesses

Marketing Conclusions

_____

_____

_____

_____

Form E8: Traffic Generator Profile

Strengths and Weaknesses

Strengths	Weaknesses

Marketing Conclusions

_____

_____

_____

_____

_____

Form E9: Competitive-Analysis Profile

Strengths and Weaknesses

Strengths	Weaknesses

Marketing Conclusions

_____

_____

_____

_____

_____

Form F: Objectives/Strategies/Tactics Worksheet

(Use one sheet per quarter.)

Location _____ Date _____

Month _____

Sales Objective:

_____

_____

_____

_____

Strategies

____ # of traffic

____ # of customers

____ $ per customer

The promotional programs I will implement to achieve the above objectives are:

1. Program name _____

   a. Timing_____

   b. Budget _____

   c. Notes _____

_____

_____

2. Program name _____

   a. Timing_____

   b. Budget _____

   c. Notes _____

Form F: Objectives/Strategies/Tactics Worksheet, continued

3. Program name _____

   a. Timing_____

   b. Budget _____

   c. Notes _____

_____

Form G: Strategy Documentation Form

Create at least three tactics per objective that you have defined, and explain them in full detail.

Objective 1: _____

_____

_____

Strategy: _____

_____

_____

Tactic 1

Target audience: _____

Description (Offer/Media/Timing/Materials/Costs): _____

_____

_____

Tactic 2

Target audience: _____

Description (Offer/Media/Timing/Materials/Costs): _____

_____

_____

Tactic 3

Target audience: _____

Description (Offer/Media/Timing/Materials/Costs): _____

_____

_____

Form G: Strategy Documentation Form, continued

Objective 2: _____

_____

_____

Strategy:

_____

_____

Tactic 1

Target audience: _____

Description (Offer/Media/Timing/Materials/Costs): _____

_____

_____

Tactic 2

Target audience: _____

Description (Offer/Media/Timing/Materials/Costs): _____

_____

_____

Tactic 3

Target audience: _____

Description (Offer/Media/Timing/Materials/Costs): _____

_____

_____

Form G: Strategy Documentation Form, continued

Objective 3: _____

_____

_____

Strategy: _____

_____

_____

Tactic 1

Target audience: _____

Description (Offer/Media/Timing/Materials/Costs): _____

_____

_____

Tactic 2

Target audience: _____

Description (Offer/Media/Timing/Materials/Costs): _____

_____

_____

Tactic 3

Target audience: _____

Description (Offer/Media/Timing/Materials/Costs): _____

_____

_____

Form H: Fundraiser Opportunities

List all opportunities for fundraising efforts you can think of. This should include local charities, local chapters of national charities, and noncharity groups such as schools, clubs, sports teams, and fraternal organizations. Once you have come up with at least 25 of them, select the five that you consider the most important, most profitable, and most easily accomplished. Then find the contact information for each and implement as described in the book.

Rank/score	Opportunity/organization	Contact/ phone number	Comments

Form I: Partnership/Traffic Generator Opportunities

List at least 25 of the top retailers, restaurants, and other businesses in your area that you consider good prospects for cross-promotions (partnership promotions). Select the five that you consider the most important, most profitable, and most easily accomplished. Then find the contact information for each and implement as described in the book.

Rank/score	Opportunity/organization	Contact/ phone number	Comments

Form J1: Profit Analysis Worksheet

Increased Customer Count—Schedule A

	Low Case	Most Likely	High Case
Step 1			
A. Number of weeks in program*	wks.	wks.	wks.
Step 2			
B. Current average weekly customers*			
C. Projected percentage increase in customers			
D. Projected weekly incremental customers (line B x line C)			
E. Total program incremental customers (line D x line A)			
Step 3			
F. Current average transactions-less discount			
G. New contribution margin based on discounted sale (*) & (**)			
H. Total incremental contribution (line E x line G)			
Step 4			
I. Start-up costs			
J. Profit lost on current customers			
Step 5			
K. Total incremental profit (loss) (line H – line I & J)			
L. Weekly incremental profit (line K ÷ line A)			
M. Total break-even customers (lines I & J ÷ line G)			
N. Weeks to break-even (line M ÷ line D)			

* The numbers are the same for all cases.

** If program does not include a discount offer, use 33.3%.

If line K is a loss, a break-even cannot be calculated.

Form J2: Start-Up Cost Checklist Worksheet

Schedule B

	Number Needed	Unit Cost	Total Cost
Printed Materials			
Letterhead stationery			
Door hangers			
Fliers			
Table tents			
Posters			
Countercards			
Banners			
Invitations			
Bounceback coupons			
Club membership cards			
Coupons			
Paid Advertising			
Newspaper/magazine			
Production			
Circulation costs			
Direct mail			
Production			
Printing			
Postage			
Radio			
Production			
Time			
Premium Items			
Buttons			
Handouts			
Other			
Other			
Store decorations			
Costumes			
T-shirts			
Additional labor			
Total Start-Up Costs	n/a	n/a	$

Form J3: Profit Lost on Current Customer Worksheet

Schedule C

	Low Case	Most Likely	High Case
A. Number of weeks in program (Schedule A, line A)*	wks.	wks.	wks.
B. Total number of current weekly customers (Schedule A, line B)			
C. Percentage of current customers eligible to participate in offer*	%	%	%
D. Number of current weekly customers eligible for discount (line B x line C)*			
E. Estimated percentage that will take advantage of discount offer**	%	%	%
F. Weekly customers participating (line D x line E)			
G. Total customers participating (line F x line A)			
H. Average transaction amount	$	$	$
I. Percentage discount offered*	%	%	%
J. Lost contribution per customer (line H x line I)	$	$	$
K. Total profit lost on current customers (line J x line G)**	$	$	$

* The numbers are the same in all cases.

** This assumption can be varied.

Insert answer on line J of previous Schedule A.

Form K1: Monthly Tracker

Month _____

	Week 1	Week 2	Week 3	Week 4	Week 5	Total
This month's sales						
Actual sales						
Sales goals						
% of goal						
Last year's actual sales						
% of comp. sales						
Month to date						
Actual sales						
Sales goals						
% of goal						
Last year's actual sales						
Comp. +/-						
Traffic						
Actual traffic						
Traffic goals						
% of goal						
$ per traffic						
Last year's actual traffic						
Comp. +/-						
Transactions						
Actual transactions						
Transaction goals						
% of goal						
Average ticket						
Last year's actual transactions						
Comp. +/-						

Form K2: Yearly Tracker

Year _____

	Jan	Feb	Mar	Apr	May	Jun	Jul	Aug	Sep	Oct	Nov	Dec	Total
This year's sales													
Actual sales													
Sales goals													
% of goal													
Last year's actual sales													
% of comp. sales													
Year to date													
Actual sales													
Sales goals													
% of goal													
Last year's actual sales													
Comp. +/-													
Traffic													
Actual traffic													
Traffic goals													
% of goal													
$ per traffic													
Last year's actual traffic													
Comp. +/-													
Transactions													
Actual transactions													
Transaction goals													
% of goal													
Average ticket													
Last year's actual transactions													
Comp. +/-													

Form K3: Customer Data Form

Evening	Jan	Feb	Mar	Apr	May	Jun	Jul	Aug	Sep	Oct	Nov	Dec	Total
Sales													
Two years ago													
Last year													
% change													
This year													
% change													
Transaction count													
Two years ago													
Last year													
% change													
This year													
% change													
Average ticket													
Two years ago													
Last year													
% change													
This year													
% change													
Traffic													
Two years ago													
Last year													
% change													
This year													
% change													

Form L1: Qualitative Marketing Promotion Summary

Project/activity _____

_____

Effective dates _____

Objective _____

_____

Description _____

_____

_____

Media _____

_____

Costs _____

_____

Results _____

_____

_____

_____

Assessment and suggestions _____

_____

_____

Form L2: Qualitative Marketing History Analysis

Past promotional activity	Dates	Comments Was it successful? Results?

Appendix B

References

Absolutely Brilliant Concepts Marketing & Consulting Inc.
Tony Policci, CEO
2925 E. Riggs Road, Ste 8–123
Chandler, AZ 85249
Phone: (480) 782-1687
Fax: (480) 821-0867
www.abctnt.com

Smartleads USA
Brad Kent, CEO
33920 US 19 N Ste 269
Palm Harbor, FL 34684
Phone: (888) 795-MAIL (6245)
Fax: (727) 726-7347
www.smartleadsusa.com

Fancy Fortune Cookies
6247 Coffman Road
Indianapolis, IN 46268
Phone: (888) 776-6611 or (317) 299-8900
www.fancyfortunecookies.com

Munroe Creative Partners
Judy Munroe, President and CEO
1435 Walnut Street
Philadelphia, PA 19102
Phone: (215) 563-8080, ext. 23
Fax: (215) 563-1270

CPSIA information can be obtained
at www.ICGtesting.com
Printed in the USA
FFOW01n0507020316
21903FF